OAT CUISINE

Also available from Souvenir Press

Health and Nutrition
THE FOOD MEDICINE BIBLE by Earl Mindell
THE ANTI-AGEING BIBLE by Earl Mindell
WHEAT-FREE COOKING by Rita Greer
ANTIOXIDANT NUTRITION by Rita Greer and Dr Robert Woodward
THE BOOK OF VITAMINS AND HEALTHFOOD SUPPLEMENTS by Rita Greer and Dr Robert Woodward
RITA GREER'S VEGETARIAN COOKBOOK by Rita Greer
THE HAY DIET MADE EASY by Jackie Habgood
THE OSTEOPOROSIS PREVENTION GUIDE by Dr Sarah Brewer
SOFT OPTIONS by Rita Greer
GET WELL WITH THE HAY DIET by Jackie Habgood
PREGNANCY THE NATURAL WAY by Dr Sarah Brewer

Nature's Remedies
GINGER by Dr Stephen Fulder
OLIVE OIL by Rita Greer and Cyril Blau
ALOE VERA by Alasdair Barcroft
LAVENDER by Philippa Waring
GINKGO AND GARLIC by Nicola Peterson
SAW PALMETTO by Dr Ray Sahelian
ECHINACEA by Douglas Schar
HYPERICUM by Andrew Chevallier
SAGE by Penelope Ody
GREEN TEA by Diana Rosen

Oat Cuisine

Classic and New Recipes for Cooking and Baking with Oats

Rita Greer

SOUVENIR PRESS

First published by
Souvenir Press Ltd,
43 Great Russell Street, London WC1B 3PA

ISBN 0 285 63579 4

Typeset by Rowland Phototypesetting Ltd,
Bury St Edmunds, Suffolk

Printed in Great Britain by
The Guernsey Press Company Ltd,
Guernsey, Channel Islands

Acknowledgements

My thanks to Mornflake Oats Ltd for information and samples of oat products, and to Quaker Oats for information.

Note to Readers

The aim of this book is to broaden the horizons for the use of oats in cooking and baking and to encourage healthy eating. Every care is taken to ensure accurate measurements/oven temperatures and methods in the recipes.

The use of hearts as symbols to grade the recipes indicates how healthy each particular recipe is and should not be taken to mean that eating the food will improve a heart condition. (For a significant health problem always seek advice at the earliest opportunity from a qualified medical practitioner.)

The publisher makes no representation, express or implied, with regard to the accuracy of the information and/or advice contained in this book, and legal responsibility or liability is not accepted by the author or the publisher for any errors or omissions that may be made or occur therein or for any loss, damage, injury or problems which may be sustained or suffered or which may in any way arise from or be consequent on the recipes offered in these pages.

Contents

CHAPTER 1

Oats

Oats are part of the family of grains we call cereals. They have been cultivated and eaten by man for thousands of years. The earliest known use has been traced back to around 3000 BC in Asia and the Ancient Greeks are known to have had porridge on the menu. By the Middle Ages it was a staple food for the British peasant.

Common oats are now grown all over the world, mostly in the cooler climes of Canada, the USA and northern Europe. There are about 25 varieties, including red oats which are more tolerant of a hot climate. Oats will grow in poor soil as long as there is enough moisture. You won't see them growing much in hot Mediterranean areas, but you will in countries like Finland and Britain, where there is no shortage of rain. Oats are grown mostly for animal feed, especially horses and sheep, but they are also a valuable and healthy food for humans.

Oats are more difficult to harvest and store than wheat, as they need more processing. If not properly treated they can taste rancid. This is due to their fatty-acid content reacting with the enzyme lipase. However, the problem can be solved by heat-treating the oats, which halts the enzyme activity.

Oats versus wheat

Oats do not have the visual glamour of wheat, 'the king of the crops'. There are no harvest fields of waving golden grain but instead what looks like rather unkempt, greyish-beige grass. Compare the two types of crop and you will see why a field of oats looks so untidy. Instead of one stem and neatly arranged wheat grains, there are many little branches off the main stalk with oat grains (in husks) at all angles.

The general preference for wheat in the diet is partly due to wheat's performance in baking, enhanced by its gluten content. Gluten is the rubbery protein that makes wheat dough so elastic, enabling it to rise, become light and hold its shape. Unfortunately the gluten found in oats does not give the same dazzling performance as that in wheat. For instance, a loaf of bread made entirely of oats is as heavy as lead, not at all like the light-textured wheat bread that we are accustomed to. Fortunately oats combine well with wheat, and a mixture of the two can be used to make excellent bread with the oats helping to keep the loaf fresh.

NUTRITION AND ENERGY

Oats play an important role in our diet as a health provider. They have a unique taste and texture and can be served in savoury or sweet food, as well as their own. This gives a wealth of opportunity for incorporating oats into the diet.

Harvesting the crop usually takes place in late August, during drier weather. The oat grains have an elongated-lemon shape with a papery outer hull which is discarded. They contain carbohydrate (73 per cent), protein (11 per cent), a little fat (9 per cent) and fibre (7 per cent). Other nutrients are iron, manganese, potassium, vitamins B1, B2, B6, folic acid and calcium. They are a good source of biotin, which acts as a vital co-enzyme for protein and carbohydrate metabolic processes. Biotin is found in every cell in the body and is termed a 'growth factor'. Deficiencies of biotin can result in retarded growth, depression and skin eruptions. Oats are the only grain which contains significant amounts of soluble fibre. It is this factor that helps to lower cholesterol levels and keep the heart healthy. However, the rest of the food eaten in the diet needs to be low in saturated fat and cholesterol for the oats to have their effect.

Some diabetics include oats in their diet regimes, as the slower release of energy is helpful for their condition. Athletes favour oats for the same reason and enjoy the sustained energy they create.

Some characteristics of oats

Adding oats to food can make it 'nuttier', chewier or softer as well as more nutritious. Oats combine well with nuts, dried fruit, raspberries, apples, wheat, barley, most herbs, cheese, mustard and fish. Some ingredients from hot countries, though, such as peppers and basil, do not seem to be comfortable with oats.

Toasting oats can make them much more exciting—it makes

them even nuttier-tasting and crisper. It also improves their colour to a warm brown.

Oats are classed as an 'unrefined cereal'. Unlike white flour and white rice, which are refined, oats have not been plundered of their nutrients by processing. They also still contain fibre, as noted above.

Oats and the coeliac

What is loosely called a 'gluten-free diet' has been prescribed for the sufferers of coeliac disease for the last fifty years or so. Wheat, rye, barley and, for most coeliacs, oats, which all contain gluten, have been forbidden. It is a difficult diet to follow but the consequences of breaking it can be most unpleasant. Sometimes the diet is broken by mistake and sometimes by a deliberate act of frustration at having to follow such a restricted regime.

After as large and important study in Scandinavia in the late 1990s, there is new thinking regarding the inclusion of oats in the coeliac diet. There is much controversy about it and no doubt it will rage on for years, but in the meantime some (not all) coeliacs are now able to introduce oats into their diet as long as they are not combined with wheat, rye or barley. This innovation can only be enjoyed with the consent of the coeliac's medical advisers. Only time will tell if the decision has been the correct one. (Suitable recipes in this book are indicated in the index.)

Oats as medicine

As oats have been used by man for many thousands of years it is no surprise to find they have been used medicinally for centuries. Although this idea would not be acceptable to modern drug-orientated medicine, it is nevertheless of historical value and of interest to those who prefer a more natural approach to health problems. (It is as well to remember that what are now called alternative therapies were once the orthodox treatment of their day.)

Oats were once a popular treatment for nervous exhaustion, stress, lethargy and depression. Rashes such as those of chicken-pox and shingles, as well as eczema and cold sores, were treated with oatmeal poultices, and oat straw was used to make a nerve tonic.

Oats as a beauty aid

As a skin cleanser oats have no rival. A face pack or scrub made from fine oatmeal and water, as a paste, can be far more effective than an expensive cleanser from the beauty counter. It is also incredibly cheap. Running the bath with oatmeal under the tap is a favoured way of coping with problem skin. A popular method is to put the oatmeal in the foot of a pair of tights. This allows the water to run through the oatmeal without ruining the bath water.

Oats and sex

Deep in our culture oats are associated with sex and are often the subject of ribald humour. 'Getting your oats' means to have sexual intercourse, but nobody knows why. By coincidence there is a link between oats and hormones. Oats in the diet help with the production of LH (luteinising hormone), which is needed for the production of testosterone, the 'male hormone' and promotes ovulation in women.

A decline in popularity

The popularity of oats as an everyday food began to decline in the middle of the twentieth century. New breakfast cereals were more exciting and convenient, as they only needed to be shaken out of the packet. People became more affluent and were not so influenced by the cheapness of oats as a food. Oats will always be associated with poverty thanks to Charles Dickens' character Oliver Twist, daring to ask for more porridge in the workhouse. (Note, he didn't ask for anything else—just more of the same.) It is no surprise to find oats on the workhouse menu because porridge is both cheap and sustaining. It was and still is used in hospitals, schools and prisons. This has given oats a strong institutional association, going back over centuries.

Oats as prison fare

'Doing porridge' means serving a prison sentence. A classic TV comedy series of the 1980s set in a prison was called just that—'Porridge'. The link between prison and porridge goes back a long way, and it is not found only in Britain. In Bridgetown, the capital of Barbados, is a small museum. One of the exhibits is a replica of a jail of centuries ago. On the cell wall is written the prisoners' diet:

Breakfast 6oz bread and 1 pint porridge
Lunch 4oz bread and 1 pint porridge
Dinner 6oz bread and 1 pint porridge

(4oz = 100g, 6oz = 170g, 1 pint = 600ml)

For a seven-day sentence, this was the food for each day. This means the week's diet included 21 pints of porridge! For a jail sentence of eight to forty-eight days the porridge ration went down to 2 pints (1.2 litres) per day and the bread allowance went up to 20oz (600g), with 1oz (25g) meat and 8oz (225g) potatoes. For a long-term jailbird the daily diet meant 25oz (700g) bread, 5oz (135g) meat (with onions and gravy), 1lb (500g) potatoes, 1 pint (600ml) of cocoa and only 1 pint of porridge.

It is interesting to note that, the longer the prison term, the less porridge the prisoners were given. The short-term prisoners consumed three times the amount given to those with long sentences to serve.

OAT PRODUCTS

All manner of products containing oats are available on the market—muesli, breakfast cereals, oatcakes, biscuits, cookies, breakfast bars, oat drinks and so on—but it is mainly the following basic oat products that are of importance in the context of oat cuisine.

Groats

Once the husk has been removed, the oat grain can be processed to make porridge oats or oatmeal. Some grains are left whole and sold as groats, either toasted or plain. They are rather mealy to eat and the plain sort need long soaking, then boiling, to make them both palatable and digestible. Plain groats can be used in flapjacks and the toasted variety are sometimes used in muesli. Their appeal is mainly to people wanting to eat 'wholefood'.

Oat bran

Two thin layers of fibre around the groat can be ground, and the result is bran. Mostly it is used for sprinkling over breakfast cereals to increase the level of fibre. It can be used in baking, but tends to make food rather dry. Some people like to use it for porridge.

Oat bran and oat germ

Oat germ is processed out of the oat grain and combined with oat bran. They are sold together as an ingredient for muesli or to sprinkle over commercial breakfast cereals.

Oatmeal

Grinding groats results in oatmeal. There are three grades—pinhead (coarse), medium and fine. Like groats, oatmeal takes a long time to cook. Purists love it as it has a more oaty taste than the more processed rolled oats, but it is more difficult to digest and takes longer to cook.

Porridge oats

These are also known as oatflakes, flaked oats, rolled oats, superfast oats, quick oats and easy oats. They are heat-treated and rolled, to flatten them. In this thinner form they can be made into porridge in four or five minutes, which is several minutes quicker than using oatmeal. It is partly this convenience feature that has helped porridge to stay so popular in the Western world.

Jumbo oats
The largest groats are rolled and flattened to make these large, thin oatflakes. The flavour is nuttier than porridge oats and they take a little longer to cook.

Small oats
These are small porridge oats.

'Instant' oats
This is the most processed of the oat products, with the oats being reduced to powder and mixed with other ingredients. By adding hot water or milk an instant porridge can be made. The result looks rather like weaning food for babies. However, it should not be given to unweaned babies as it is too difficult for them to digest. The convenience factor is the main reason for the popularity of this type of product.

Oat flour
This is rarely seen on the shop shelves, but is easily made at home by grinding rolled oats in an electric coffee grinder. The result is a greyish flour for baking, thickening and dusting.

Oat 'milk'
Oats can be processed to make a kind of milk. It is popular with vegans, who don't take animal products in their strict diet. Flavoured varieties are sold as 'oat drinks' labelled 'non-dairy'. Vanilla, cocoa and fruit are often used as flavourings.

Shopping and storage

The famous named brands will always be the best buy for quality. Supermarket 'own label' will usually be cheaper but not necessarily as good. Oatmeals, groats, oat bran and oat germ can be bought at health stores. Porridge oats can be bought at supermarkets and smaller food shops or health stores. Oat drinks are most likely to be found at health stores, which cater for vegan and non-dairy diets such as those for people with milk allergies.

Avoid storing oats for too long, as they do not keep so well as wheat flour. If you have not used up an opened packet of oats or oatmeal in three months, throw it away and buy fresh. There is no point in buying large amounts just to store them—buy little and often and store in a cool, dry place.

Horse sense

Talk to anyone who knows about horses, and they will enthuse about oats as equine food. In the racing world oats are a big issue, as the feeding of thoroughbreds to obtain the best performance is a priority. Jenny Pitman, a top trainer of National Hunt horses, favours bruised oats. She always had samples analysed before purchasing. She would select two or three of the best, put a handful of each into separate plastic bags and weigh them on the kitchen scales. The heaviest would be chosen, because the best weight would indicate the best food value. However, she left the final choice to the horses themselves. Two samples of oats that she had selected would be put in two little heaps, equidistant from a horse in his stable. After sniffing both samples, the horse would automatically eat the most nutritious one. And that is the one that would be ordered from the feed merchant.

Humans don't have this talent, and will eat any food if its appearance attracts them. We know about nutrition, we know what we should be eating, and then we persistently eat all the wrong things. At least with oats we know they are a wonderful food and that we can benefit our health by eating them.

The new recipes in this book will widen your scope for cooking and baking with oats, while the classic recipes will give you tasty food that has stood the test of time. Between them, you will be able to increase your consumption of oats and, as a result, enjoy the benefits of better health.

CHAPTER 2

Oats in a Healthy Diet

The last fifty years or so have been a time of plenty. Shortages of foodstuffs are now rare. We have canned, dried, chilled, frozen and fresh food—and plenty of it. People in the Western world are not starving, yet many are not properly fed. We all expect to live to a good old age, but few of us will enjoy good health if we do. The fact is that the average Western diet gets worse by the year. The balance is wrong—there is too much fat, sugar and salt and not enough fibre, fresh vegetables and fruit.

Much of this sorry state of affairs is due to lack of knowledge about nutrition. Oats have an important part to play in a good diet if people understand their value as a highly nutritious and versatile food.

WHY IT WENT WRONG

The wild abandon with cooking ingredients that we have seen since the 1950s has been a backlash against the shortages during the Second World War, followed by rationing. It has resulted in the overuse of cream, cheese, sugar, butter, lard, white flour and processed foods. This has been encouraged by TV 'celebrity' chefs and cooks, who show no restraint as their prime object is to entertain. With colour printing and photography having improved beyond all bounds, the result has been an abundance of cookbooks that are little more than a series of lavish photographs with the minimum amount of text. Health food doesn't seem to feature much on today's cookery scene, probably because most people do not fully appreciate the value of good health. The connection between health and food intake is constantly played down by the media and by advertisers.

But changes are afoot. Who would have thought organic foods would have come to be in such demand?

Changing times

Times have changed a great deal over the last hundred years, nowhere more than in the kitchen. Where there were once little armies of servants to prepare and cook the food, see to the washing-up, wait at table, organise provisions and generally cater for their employers' eating habits, nowadays we want less fuss, less work in the kitchen and smaller menus. As there are now no servants and only high-tech equipment, this seems like common sense. Why else would we accept the microwave and the ready meal?

YOUR BODY'S REMARKABLE FOOD-PROCESSING MACHINE

In order to find out how oats can help you to better health, you need to look broadly at your food intake to see how they can be incorporated. Firstly, you need to be aware of a few facts about food—why some foods are good for us, why others are not, and what happens when we get the balance wrong.

The human body possesses a truly remarkable system for

processing food, sorting it out, disposing of what it doesn't need, and using what it does need for maintenance and repair, for energy to move and work, for growth and (sometimes) reproduction. If the supply of food diminishes beyond a certain point, the system raids the body's own fat stores and even lean tissue. If the supply of food ceases altogether and there are no stores left to raid, the result is eventually death. For the body, food is a serious business.

Digestion enables some foods to be processed into more basic kinds of food or treated chemically within the body. Others require less drastic treatment, and some food can pass through the body practically unchanged.

Basics

Basic foods for a Western 'mixed diet' are meat, fish, eggs, milk and dairy foods, cereals (grains), fats and oils, vegetables, fruit, nuts, sugar and beverages. Within these foods are a variety of components—proteins, carbohydrates, saturated and unsaturated fats and oils, cholesterol, vitamins, minerals and trace elements.

FOODS FOR REPAIR AND MAINTENANCE

Being such a miracle of engineering, to keep going your body needs to be able to extract certain substances from its food to repair wear and tear and keep it running smoothly. It needs protein for rebuilding and repair, and it can extract this mainly from meat, fish, eggs, cheese, nuts, beans, peas, potatoes and bread. In Britain people usually have too much protein in their food, with most of it coming from meat. Oats can have a part to play in providing some protein: 2oz (50g) of porridge oats, for instance, contain over 5g of protein. Vegetarians and vegans find this more valuable than meat and fish eaters as they have fewer sources of protein.

FOODS FOR ENERGY

By using the energy factor in certain foods, your body can convert it into fuel for the efficient running of its many parts. It burns up this fuel as it works. This is why foods are measured by their energy value—calories. Starchy foods contain a high proportion of carbohydrate. Among the starchiest foods in the British diet are bread, potatoes, flour, rice, pasta and root vegetables—all high in calories. Two ounces (50g) of porridge oats have 31g of carbohydrate.

Sugar

One substance that is pure carbohydrate is sugar, and the average person eats too much of it. When taken into the body in large amounts (such as in sweets, chocolate, cakes and biscuits), this can pose a problem in the fuel department. The system becomes overloaded with sugar, and as too much of it is transferred into the blood it can cause internal uproar. Then, when the sugar level suddenly falls again, the power fades and a rather jerky supply of energy is the result.

A steady flow of energy is much better for body function, and this is best maintained by eating foods such as fruit, bread, pasta, rice and oats which contain other substances as well, instead of just eating pure carbohydrate (sugar). Your body has a natural way of keeping the supply of energy constant and does not need boosts of sugar. It can take fat out of the body's many fat stores and convert it to energy, as needed. Not only can it extract from the foods eaten the fat needed for the stores, but it can actually make fat for storage out of excess intakes of proteins and carbohydrate.

FATS AND OILS

A diet without any fat or oil can be extremely dangerous. Certain vitamins can only be used by the body in conjunction with fats. People on slimming diets which cut down too drastically on fats risk damaging their health.

The gourmet can eat a large quantity of fat at one sitting. So too can the lorry driver at a transport café. Schoolchildren who eat chips with everything and top up with ice-cream, chocolate bars, cakes and biscuits are eating a high-fat diet. It is not just a question of the fat you can see such as the packs of butter and margarine and bottles of cooking oil, but the hidden fat in the ice-cream, cheeses, salad dressings, cakes, biscuits, pastry, eggs, confectionery, chips, pizza, flours and fried foods.

If your body takes in too much food (of all kinds) it will convert what it does not need at that particular time into storage fat for use as a future supply of energy. It can store it in all kinds of places—under the skin, around the heart and other organs, inside the arteries, around the waist, hips and thighs. Really fat people, called 'obese', may carry many kilos of stores fat around with them, straining the skeleton, the heart and the lungs, clogging up the arteries and making breathing difficult. This is not only dangerous to health, but a very uncomfortable energy stockpile.

The fats and oils used in cooking are a mixture of three main types of fat plus a few more obscure ones. Depending on the kind of oil or fat, the proportions of the main types they contain vary. These three main types are saturated fat, mono-unsaturated fat and polyunsaturated fat. Those fats and oils with a high level of saturated fat are loosely referred to as 'saturated fats' even though they contain other fats as well. The ones with high levels of polyunsaturated fat are generally called 'unsaturated fats' or 'polyunsaturated fats' even though they contain some saturated fat too.

We need both saturated and polyunsaturated fat in our food. Ideally we should eat more polyunsaturated fat than saturated, as polyunsaturated fat contains 'essential fatty acids'. As their name suggests, they are essential for health. Although we can make our own saturated fat in the body, we cannot make our own polyunsaturated fat—that is, we must eat it to obtain it.

Saturated fats

The following contain high levels of saturated fat: coconut oil, cream, butter, suet, palm oil, hard margarine, and hard block vegetable oils. Coconut and palm oil are widely used in margarines and ice-cream as well as in the bakery trade. You can see from the list that both animal fats and vegetable oils can be saturated.

Polyunsaturated fats

The following contain high levels of polyunsaturated fat: safflower seed oil, sunflower seed oil, soya oil, corn (maize) oil. Polyunsaturated margarines—that is, those high in polyunsaturates—contain around 55 per cent polyunsaturated and 25 per cent saturated fat. Egg yolks contain both saturated and polyunsaturated fat. Olive oil is the odd man out in the fat league, with low levels of both saturated and polyunsaturated fat, but a high level of mono-unsaturated fat. Other sources of fat or oil in the diet are meat, fish, vegetables, nuts and seeds. We even get a little from grains, too.

Cholesterol

Cholesterol is a substance rather like fat, found in animals. (It is never found in plants.) It is thought to play a part in causing heart disease, as it can build up in our blood to unhealthy levels. However, there is much controversy over the idea among the experts, who disagree wildly about its dangers.

The main sources of cholesterol in our diet are meat, egg yolks, lard, cheeses, milk, cream, butter and suet. We also get a little in fish. By eating foods which are *low* in animal fat we can cut down easily on the amount of cholesterol we take in. This is a good idea as our bodies can make their own cholesterol, anyway.

The processing of fats and oils

By a process called 'hydrogenation' manufacturers can make a naturally unsaturated oil into a saturated one. This helps to preserve it, and solid blocks of vegetable oil for frying have usually been treated this way. Manufacturers can also add substances to fats which would normally go hard in the fridge to make them stay soft for spreading. This tends to confuse people, who may associate soft margarines with ones that contain a high level of polyunsaturates. Cream is now added to some brands of butter to make them softer and easier to spread. The lesson to be learned here is not to assume that a soft fat is high in polyunsaturated fat or that vegetables fats are necessarily healthier than animal fats, as both can be very saturated.

FOODS FOR CLEANSING AND WASTE DISPOSAL

This is a very important department, which needs water and fibre to carry out its duties. The main purpose of the cleansing and waste-disposal system is to keep food on the move, cleaning the food canal as it goes, collecting all the debris and unwanted food that cannot be reused or stored, and organising its regular disposal from the body. The best fibre for this is cereal fibre, and it is found in wholewheat flour and bread. Brown rice, potato skins, root vegetables, leafy greens, peas, beans and fruit are other sources of fibre which can help with the work. Oats are the only grain which contains significant amounts of both soluble and insoluble fibre. It is soluble fibre which helps to lower cholesterol levels and keep your heart healthy.

If your body takes in too much fibre, the cleansing and waste-disposal department goes into overdrive and works too fast. In the mad dash to cope, food which would normally go for storage gets swept out with the rubbish, as your body doesn't have time to process it properly. (This is how high-fibre slimming diets work.)

If your body doesn't get enough fibre, on the other hand, the cleansing and waste-disposal department organises a go-slow or even a strike. The gloomy result is constipation. Years of constipation can result in the formation of extra little storage departments for waste—rubbish waiting to be disposed of—the condition known as diverticulitis. Carrying waste around inside the body is not only uncomfortable but it also gives a home to all kinds of harmful bacteria, bent on causing disease. Food should ideally take no more than about 36 hours to be processed and pass right through the body. For people who suffer from constipation this may take anything up to 14 days. You can see from these facts just how important it is to consume enough fibre in your food. If you eat sensibly, though, there is no need to take extra bran as there will be quite enough for the job in a healthy diet. Most people in Britain probably need about 1½oz (35g) of fibre per day but are getting only about ¾oz (20g).

The husk from oats is processed to produce oat bran. You will find it at the supermarket on the breakfast cereals shelves. Sprinkled over cereal, it is a popular way of putting extra bran into the diet.

ORGANISERS AND SPECIAL AGENTS

There are lots of special jobs that need to be done on food as it passes through the food canal inside the body. With every mouthful, hopefully, there comes a fresh shift of workers—vitamins and minerals and trace elements—to help organise the food-processing, carry oxygen, lubricate the body cells, keep the nervous system going, strengthen the skin, heal wounds, prevent infection and illness, look after the hair, teeth and nails, and generally keep the human body in running order and in a healthy state.

This army of special agents is very vulnerable, as cooking and the processing of food can destroy many of them. Raw fresh foods contain the highest number. Eating too much highly processed and 'junk' food can threaten our health because the precious vitamins and minerals are wasted in the food's processing. Going without the right nutrients for long periods can have bad effects. The result can be a whole legion of niggling or serious disorders, illness and disease.

VITAMINS AND MINERALS

Some vitamin D can be made by the body after exposure to sunshine. Vitamins A, D, E and F are built into fats and are found in animal and fish oils. Other excellent sources of vitamins and minerals are fruit and vegetables (fresh). A few vitamins and minerals can be stored in the body, but most need to be taken in regularly. The worst source of supply is junk food and processed 'convenience foods', in which they have largely been destroyed. These are some of the important vitamins and minerals and the parts of the body they service:

VITAMINS

Vitamin A for healthy bones, hair, eyes, skin, teeth
Vitamin B complex (*B1*, *B2*, *B6*, *B12*) for healthy eyes, food canal, hair, brain, ears, heart, nervous system, nails, liver, skin, blood, muscles, gall bladder, glands, tongue
Biotin for cell growth, for making fat, for helping to use protein, fat and carbohydrate in the body
Choline for a healthy liver, gall bladder and nerves
Folic acid for the appetite, reproduction, circulation, liver function, red blood cell formation
Inositol for helping to stop the arteries hardening, for reducing cholesterol, for helping the body to use fat and grow hair
Niacin for healthy circulation, for sex hormone production, for helping the body to use protein, fat and carbohydrate
PABA (*para-aminobenzoic acid*): for healthy hair and skin
Pangamic acid for assisting breathing and encouraging the

glands nervous system to work, and helping the body to use protein, fat and sugar
Pantothenic acid for helping to remove toxic substances, for possibly helping hair to keep its colour, for activating friendly bacteria in the food canal, and helping the body to use protein
Vitamin C for healthy adrenal glands, blood, skin, ligaments, bones, gums, heart, teeth
Vitamin D for healthy bones, heart, nerves, skin, teeth, thyroid gland
Vitamin E for healthy blood vessels, heart, lungs, nerves, skin
Vitamin F for healthy cells, glands, hair, nerves, skin
Vitamin K for healthy blood and liver
Vitamin P (bioflavonoids) for healthy blood, skin, gums, ligaments, bones, teeth

MINERALS

Calcium for healthy bones, blood, heart, skin, teeth
Chromium for blood circulation
Copper for healthy blood, bones, circulation, hair, skin
Iodine for hair, nails, skin, teeth, thyroid gland
Iron for healthy blood, bones, nails and skin
Magnesium for healthy arteries, bones, heart, muscles, nerves, teeth
Manganese for healthy brain, muscles, nerves
Phosphorus for healthy bones, blood, brain, nerves, teeth
Potassium for healthy blood, heart, kidneys, muscles, nerves, skin
Selenium for a healthy pancreas
Sodium for healthy blood, muscles, nerves
Zinc for healthy blood, heart

Good sources of vitamins
Vitamin A: fish, fish liver oil, green and yellow fruit and vegetables, carrots, spinach

Vitamin B1: brewer's yeast, wheatgerm, wholegrains including oats, yoghurt
Vitamin B2: brewer's yeast, eggs, fruit, green vegetable leaves, beans, nuts, wholegrains including oats, poultry
Vitamin B6: avocado pear, bananas, brewer's yeast, cabbage, fish, green vegetable leaves, prunes, raisins, walnuts, wheatgerm
Vitamin B12: beef, eggs, milk products, fish, pork, cottage cheese
Biotin: brewer's yeast, egg yolk, beans, wholegrains, oats
Choline: brewer's yeast, egg yolk, fish, beans, soya, wheatgerm
Folic acid: oranges, lemons, eggs, green vegetable leaves, milk products, seafood, wholegrains
Inositol: brewer's yeast, oranges, lemons, meat, milk, nuts, vegetables, wholegrains
Niacin: eggs, lean meat, milk products, poultry, seafood, wholewheat bread and cereals
PABA (*para-aminobenzoic acid*): wheat bran, brewer's yeast, eggs, liver, milk, rice, wheatgerm
Pangamic acid: brewer's yeast, brown rice, sunflower and sesame seeds, wholegrains
Pantothenic acid: brewer's yeast, eggs, beans, mushrooms, salmon, wheatgerm, wholegrains
Vitamin C: fresh fruit and vegetables
Vitamin D: egg yolk, milk, fish, fishbones
Vitamin E: butter, dark-green vegetable leaves (e.g. kale, spinach), eggs, fruit, nuts, vegetable oils, wheatgerm
Vitamin F: safflower, sunflower, corn and soya oils; wheatgerm, sunflower seeds
Vitamin K: green vegetable leaves, safflower oil, yoghurt, oats
Vitamin P: fruits including skin—apricots, grapes, cherries, grapefruit, plums, lemons

Good sources of minerals
Calcium: milk, cheese, yoghurt, almonds
Chromium: brewer's yeast, corn oil, wholegrain cereals

Copper: beans, nuts, seafood, raisins, avocado, liver, soya, beansprouts, watercress, parsley
Iodine: seafood, seaweed
Iron: eggs, fish, wheatgerm, poultry, liver, dark-green vegetables, spices
Magnesium: wheat bran, honey, green vegetables, nuts
Manganese: bananas, wheat bran, celery, cereals including oats, egg yolks, green vegetable leaves, beans, liver, nuts, wholegrains, pineapple
Phosphorus: eggs, fish, grains including oats, meat, poultry, liver
Potassium: dates, figs, peaches, tomatoes, raisins, seafood, sunflower seeds, fresh vegetables, fresh fruit
Selenium: fish, meat, eggs, wholegrains, brown rice
Sodium: salt, milk, cheese, seafood
Zinc: brewer's yeast, liver, seafood, soya, mushrooms, sunflower seeds, spinach

All these are important for our health, but there are two minerals about which you should know a little more—salt and potassium.

Salt

One of the most important minerals in the body is sodium. It is in our bones, body cells and bloodstream. All foods contain some sodium naturally. And we are also great users of salt, which contain 40 per cent sodium. It is a cheap ingredient and plentiful, and we use it liberally in cooking and at table to bring out the flavour of food. Manufacturers use it with a heavy hand in processed food, both to preserve and to flavour it. In very rare circumstances people fail to take enough salt for the level of their physical activity. The result can be low blood pressure, rapid pulse and cramps. By taking salt and water the situation can soon be put right.

Most of us, though, take too much salt in or on our food.

The results of this can be serious—hypertension (high blood pressure) leading to strokes, and heart and kidney disease. It may even lead to heart attacks.

While the body is usually able to dispose of some excess sodium via the kidneys and by sweating and weeping, sodium can reach a level at which the body cannot cope. Eating too much salt makes us thirsty. This encourages drinking too much liquid—tea, coffee, beer etc.—and the result can be oedema (water retention). (For this doctors prescribe diuretic drugs to make the kidneys work harder to get rid of the salt and water. This seems to be a rather drastic way of coping with a problem which could often be solved by asking the patient to reduce his or her salt intake.)

The truth of the matter is that we do not need the salt we add in cooking and at table. By adding it to the natural sodium that exists in all our foods as well as the salt in the processed food we eat, we are possibly giving our bodies long-term health problems. The fact is that most of us take 20 or 30 times too much salt for our needs.

Potassium

There is another mineral, closely associated with sodium. This is potassium, and it is found in the tissues of our muscles. Most of us eat far too few of the right foods to give us the potassium we need. Some of us only get as little as a quarter of what we should have. The best source is fresh vegetables. A poor source is overcooked vegetables and highly processed foods.

Salt and potassium form a balance in our bodies. Because we take too much salt and too little potassium most of us have an incorrect balance of the two. Increasing the amount of potassium in the diet can be easily done by eating more unprocessed fruit and vegetables.

Water

Water, although it is not a food, is essential for life. It accounts for two-thirds of our body weight, and our bodies cannot function without it. Next to air for breathing, water is the most important thing for survival and we can last only a matter of days without it. We take in water in drinks such as tea, coffee and beer, and also in foods. We lose it in sweat and tears, in our breath and via the kidneys.

THE 'BALANCED DIET'

Nobody knows exactly what the 'balanced diet' is, although nutritionists and dietitians have been prattling on about it for decades. The chart on pages 24 and 25 gives you some sort of guide as to what you ought to be eating each day. But remember that it is a very basic guide, nothing more.

Some people may like to add to this list 1 tablespoon of bran to increase fibre intake; plus one glass of wine for women, and two for men. Some items, such as beer and spirits, are outside the guide. Other items to avoid are high-fat, high-salt snack foods, high-sugar drinks, and high-fat foods with double cream. However, we would not be human if we didn't kick over the traces now and then—but not *every* day! Leave treats for special occasions.

A diet high in starch-rich foods like oats can result in lower cholesterol, but the diet must also be low in fat for it to be effective. Spreading margarine or butter thickly on toast or vegetables is a bad habit. Frying instead of grilling is also a bad habit.

Trends

Trends in diet and eating habits are getting worse. We have a wide range of foods to choose from every day. Stores are open 24 hours a day, seven days a week. Unfortunately, what they sell most of is junk food.

In some ways we don't have as wide a variety of food as

Basic daily guide: foods for a healthy mixed diet

Types of food	*Total amount*	*Choose from*
high carbo-hydrates	3–4 portions	wholegrain breads, pasta, rice, oats, potatoes, dumplings, crispbreads, pancakes, porridge or cereal, pizza (base), plain biscuits e.g. oatcakes
'greens'	1–2 portions	green cabbage, spinach, kale, spring greens, green lettuce, watercress etc.
other fresh vegetables	4 portions	carrots, onions, peas, green beans, leeks, parsnips, turnips, swede, celeriac, courgettes, peppers, tomatoes, salad vegetables
fresh fruit	3 portions	apples, oranges, pears, bananas, pineapple, grapes, berry fruits, peaches, apricots, plums, melon, soft fruits, kiwi-fruit etc.
high proteins	2 portions	meat, fish, low-fat cheeses, TVP (texturised vegetable protein), beans, tofu, nuts
fats and oils	2 tablespoons	sunflower oil, extra-virgin olive oil, polyunsaturated soft margarine, butter (a little)

Types of food	*Total amount*	*Choose from*
sugar	1 tablespoon	sugar, jam, honey, golden syrup
milk	¼ pint (150ml)	low-fat milk or half-fat milk
treats	1 small portion	biscuit, cake, chocolate, sweets, snacks

our ancestors had. Over 160 different grains and seeds have been whittled down to a handful, with just one main one—wheat. Wheat breakfast cereal, wheat biscuits for elevenses, wheat pizza or pie for lunch, wheat cakes for tea, wheat pasta for dinner, wheat biscuits for a bedtime snack. By coincidence, the major allergen in the UK is wheat . . .

Heart grading ♡♡♡♡♡

Cutting down on wheat and increasing your intake of oats would seem to be a good idea. But how will you know which oat-based foods are the healthiest? Each recipe in this book is graded with from one to five hearts—the more hearts there are, the healthier the recipe. I have chosen a heart symbol because a healthy heart is the key to overall health. Hearts have been deducted where there is more fat (butter, cream, margarine, oil), more sugar (treacle, sugars, honey), and less fibre. All the recipes set out to have low levels of salt, or none at all.

Life would be pretty dull if we just ate porridge (four hearts) for every meal. Fortunately, there is a wide range of savoury, semi-sweet and sweet food made with oats, to fill the gap between breakfast and bedtime, with good heart scores. Sometimes, just now and then, we need to break the rules for a celebration. But it is no coincidence that festive food scores low on hearts. You will find that ice-cream made with oats, for example, scores only one heart. The recipe is included, nevertheless, because it is a delicious treat, and because it is just one of a range of recipes that illustrate the versatility of oats. Flapjacks too are high in sugar and fat, so they also score low on hearts. Oat breads score high, but if you spread them lavishly with butter or margarine hearts will need to be deducted. Use the hearts in this book to guide you to the healthiest foods to be eaten most often. From time to time use the recipes with lower scores as treats but go easy on them. In other words, take care of your health by eating well.

CHAPTER 3

Breakfasts

OATIES ♡♡♡♡♡

A 'smoothie' is a liquid food made by blending fruit, fruit juice and yoghurt. An 'oatie' is a smoothie plus oats. Originally a breakfast food for the open air and a spin-off from the milkshake, oaties are now the favourite fast food of people in a rush. They are a healthy supernutritional food—but slow sipping is recommended (as opposed to fast gulping).

Raspberry Oatie (1 serving)

- 1 banana, sliced
- 6 fresh raspberries
- 1 level tablespoon porridge oats
- 1 heaped tablespoon set natural yoghurt or 1½ tablespoons liquid yoghurt
- ¼pt (150ml) (non-fizzy) apple juice

Method: Put all ingredients into a blender. Liquidise until smooth. Serve in a tall glass, freshly made.

NOTE: If your blender goblet is made of toughened glass you will be able to use frozen fruit (straight from the freezer). However, if it is plastic it is advisable to use fresh or defrosted fruit, to avoid damage.

Peach Oatie
Omit raspberries and substitute ½ peeled and stoned ripe peach, chopped.

Pineapple Oatie
Omit raspberries and substitute 1 slice fresh, ripe pineapple, chopped.

Blackberry Oatie
Omit raspberries and substitute 8 fresh blackberries.

Plum Oatie
Omit raspberries and substitute 2 ripe plums, peeled and stoned.

OAT BREAKFAST FLAKES

Breakfast cereal doesn't have to come out of a packet. Instead, make these quick and easy breakfast flakes yourself. Eat them on their own freshly baked with skimmed milk, or top with fresh fruit such as chopped strawberries, raspberries or sliced banana. Porridge and muesli haters could easily be seduced by this delicious breakfast. Here are three versions:

Oat and Honey Breakfast Flakes (makes 1 serving, or 2 with fruit) ♡♡♡♡

1oz (25g) porridge oats
1 slightly heaped teaspoon runny honey
1 level teaspoon caster sugar
1 pinch salt
4 tablespoons water

Preheat oven: Gas 8/450°F/230°C/fan oven 210°C

Position: top shelf
Baking time: about 7 minutes/fan oven 5 minutes

Method: Grind the oats to a fine flour in a coffee grinder. Put into a basin with the remaining ingredients and mix/beat to a smooth, thin batter. Have ready a large greased baking sheet. Leaving space between, put little blobs of the batter on the sheet. (A teaspoon will make 3.) Bake until brown round the edges. Loosen with a spatula and leave on a plate to cool for 5 minutes. Serves as suggested above.

Malted Oat Breakfast Flakes (makes 1 serving, or 2 with fruit) ♡♡♡♡

1oz (25g) porridge oats
1 level teaspoon malt extract
pinch salt
4 tablespoons cold water

Method: As for oat and honey breakfast flakes. Bake until crisp and golden. Eat freshly baked as suggested above.

Oat and Nut Breakfast Flakes (makes 2 servings, or 3 with fruit) ♡♡♡♡

1oz (25g) porridge oats
1 slightly heaped teaspoon ground mixed nuts
1 slightly heaped teaspoon caster sugar
1 level teaspoon sesame seeds
1 level teaspoon malt extract or runny honey
pinch salt
4 tablespoons cold water

Method: As for oat and honey breakfast flakes. Eat freshly baked as suggested above.

PORRIDGE

Oats or oatmeal cooked with water or milk and served with a sweetening and milk or cream equals 'porridge'. It is all credit to oats that porridge is equally at home served in the dining-room from a silver tray or out of a blackened old pot by the camp fire.

Some people enjoy porridge—others loathe it. Usually, how

people feel about it has something to do with childhood memories. Was the porridge they remember smooth and golden, or grey, thick and lumpy? Obviously, smooth porridge served with brown sugar, runny honey or golden syrup will harbour happier memories than a grey stodge with lumps that came thudding off the spoon. (In Scotland it is not unknown for thick porridge to be poured into an empty drawer, allowed to cool and then be cut into slices and used instead of bread.) However it is served up, the simple dish that is porridge needs to be made without lumps. And as the manufacturers of porridge oats are shy on the subject of lumps, it must be dealt with here.

The problem can start when the oats meet the liquid. Small, soft lumps may form because some of the oats stick together. Stirring and heating can have the effect of making the lumps larger and more solid. No cook who makes lumpy porridge is a cook to be admired! It rates with not being able to boil an egg, another simple dish which can end in disappointment for the eater and a bad reputation for the cook.

Avoiding lumps
Lumpy porridge can be averted at the initial mixing stage. Put the cold water into the pan. Sprinkle in the oats, rather than putting them in all in one go. Next, with clean hands, stir and agitate the oats with your fingers, feeling for any potential lumps. Rub between thumb and fingers to disperse. Then proceed to cook and stir (or microwave). If any lumps survive after the porridge is made, remove with a spoon and discard.

Plain Porridge (2 servings) ♡♡♡♡

2oz (50g) or 5 heaped tablespoons
2¼ cups cold water (or skimmed milk and water mixed)

Method: Put the oats and water into a small saucepan. Get out any lumps (see above) and bring gently to the boil. Simmer for 4 minutes while you stir. Turn into 2 bowls. Serve hot, with a little skimmed milk and sprinkled with demerara sugar.

Microwave Porridge (2 servings) ♡♡♡♡

Use the same ingredients as for plain porridge. Mix in a large microwavable bowl, removing any lumps (see above). *Do not cover.* Cook on full power according to your microwave (see manufacturer's instructions). Leave to stand for 2 minutes, then stir and serve as for plain porridge.

Cooking times/settings

2 servings: 650w for 6 minutes
or 800w for 4½ minutes

1 serving: 650w for 3 minutes
or 800w for 2½ minutes

For one serving use 1oz (25g) porridge oats and just over 1 cup of cold water.

Quick Porridge (2 servings) ♡♡♡♡

Sometimes it is the coarse texture of porridge that puts people off. There are also certain people who, for one reason or another, are unable to chew. Use the plain porridge recipe but grind the oats to flour in a coffee grinder first. Cook for much less time, e.g. 1 minute instead of 4.

Gourmet Porridge (2 servings) ♡♡♡

Even the gourmet will appreciate porridge if the very best quality ingredients are used and its presentation is stylish and attractive. Use the plain porridge recipe but choose best organic oats and (still) spring water. Serve with single cream and demerara sugar. Bone china porridge bowls and silver spoons would present it nicely!

Oatmeal Porridge (2 servings) ♡♡♡♡

½pt (300ml) cold water
pinch salt
2oz (50g) medium oatmeal

Method: Bring the water and salt to the boil in a small saucepan. Hold the oatmeal in your palm with the fingers closed over it. Allow a thin stream of oatmeal to trickle into the boiling water while you stir. Bring to the boil again and continue to cook/stir for about 10 minutes. Pour into porridge bowls and leave to cool a little and thicken. Serve with skimmed milk and brown sugar or runny honey to taste.

NOTE: Some people prefer a longer cooking time, up to 20 minutes. Cook over a very gentle heat, stirring from time to time, if using this method.

Chocolate Porridge (1 serving) ♡♡♡

The kind of person who cannot contemplate eating plain porridge may enthuse about this brown version, and vice versa. It might just persuade the porridge-hating child to a change of heart. However, it would be unwise to serve it to someone who doesn't like the idea of it.

2 heaped tablespoons porridge oats
1 tablespoon low-fat dried milk granules
few drops vanilla flavouring
6oz (175ml) water
1 level teaspoon sugar (or more to taste)
1 slightly heaped teaspoon cocoa powder

Method: Make the oats into flour using a coffee grinder. Put into a small non-stick saucepan with the remaining ingredients. Stir and remove any lumps. Bring to the boil, stirring all the time with a wooden spoon. Simmer for 1 minute, then turn into a serving bowl. Pour a little low-fat milk around the edge and serve immediately.

NOTE: If the cocoa looks lumpy put it into the saucepan through a wire sieve.

MUESLI

Muesli is really a cold form of porridge with extras— fruit, nuts, seeds, sweetening, and liquid to moisten. The first muesli was formulated to match the nutritional value of 'mother's milk' (human breast milk) by Dr Bircher-Benner in the last century for use in his Swiss clinic. He called it 'raw fruit porridge', and his recipe—♡♡♡♡♡—was as follows:

- 1 tablespoon medium oatmeal or rolled oats, soaked overnight in water
- 1 tablespoon fresh lemon juice
- 3 tablespoons raw milk
- 1 tablespoon hazelnuts or almonds
- 2 eating-apples, grated

The ingredients were simply mixed together in a bowl and served to patients. It was a far cry from what they were used to—sizzling bacon and kidneys, sausages, ham, cheeses, rolls and butter . . .

Modern mueslis have taken on quite a different form and enjoy a fair share of the commercial breakfast cereal market. (Dr Bircher-Benner must be spinning in his grave at some of the results of the industry's creative muesli formulas!) It is easy to see how muesli has achieved a cult food status, being entirely different from the traditional cooked breakfast or single-grain cereal. It looks more intriguing and is associated with good health. It can be infinitely varied to suit the individual, and made quickly, leaving little in the way of washing-up.

No cooking or cooking skills are required, and sprinkling is a quiet activity so there is no noisy food processor. No wonder it is popular. Commercial brands of muesli don't vary from one batch to the next and usually comprise oats, nuts, dried fruit and seeds. At home things are different, and no two mueslis are the same. The oat base is mixed with fresh and dried fruit, nuts, seeds, honey or sugar, milk or fruit juice and sometimes yoghurt, wheatgerm and bran. Home, or commercial, the basis of muesli is oats and this has not changed since muesli was first invented.

A modest modern muesli would be oats, grated apple, sultanas, chopped mixed nuts, milk and brown sugar. However, with such a wide range of ingredients readily available on the supermarket and health-store shelves, many more ingredients can be incorporated, some quite ordinary and others more exotic. The temptation is to make a lavish concoction with too many ingredients and a confusion of tastes and textures. Oats, 1 fresh fruit, 1 dried fruit, 1 type of seed or nut, 1 sweetening and 1 liquid are quite sufficient. Choose from the lists that follow:

Ripe fresh fruit

eating-apple*
banana
blueberries
seedless grapes
kiwi-fruit
mango
melon
nectarine*
pawpaw (papaya)
dessert pear*
pineapple
plums*
raspberries
strawberries

*Purists will leave the skin on these.

Dried fruit

chopped dried apricots
sliced stoned dates
guavas
mango
nectarines
pawpaw
peaches
raisins
sultanas

'Ready-to-eat' dried fruit is eminently suitable.

Shelled nuts and seeds

almonds
brazils
cashews
hazelnuts
pinenuts
pistachios
pumpkin seeds
sesame seeds
sunflower seeds
walnuts

Avoid peanuts.

Brans etc.

oat bran
wheat bran
wheatgerm

Liquids to moisten

non-fizzy apple juice
skimmed milk
orange juice
pineapple juice
soya milk
low-fat yoghurt (plain)

Purists will opt for freshly made juice.

By adding a bran the fibre content of the muesli will be raised; by adding wheatgerm the protein content is given a boost. Too many nuts will put the fat content up, and too much honey or brown sugar will result in a dish that is too sweet. Aim for a semi-sweet muesli that is well balanced.

Serious home muesli makers store their ingredients in jars in the kitchen and select their choice of the day as their fancy takes them. The less serious buy commercially made muesli and just add milk. To cut down on the number of storage jars in use you can make up muesli bases for regular use. Just add the fresh fruit of your choice and sweeten and moisten to suit. Here are three options, ranging from the modest, through the more adventurous to the ultimate.

Simple Muesli Base ♡♡♡♡

- 8 heaped tablespoons porridge oats
- 4 heaped tablespoons chopped mixed nuts (avoid peanuts)
- 2 heaped tablespoons raisins or sultanas

Mix all the ingredients in a bowl and transfer to a storage jar. Use 2 or 3 heaped tablespoons of the mixture and combine with grated or chopped raw apple or banana. Sweeten with a little brown sugar or honey and moisten with milk.

Medium Muesli Base ♡♡♡♡

- 8 heaped tablespoons porridge oats
- 4 heaped tablespoons chopped mixed nuts (avoid peanuts)
- 2 or 3 heaped tablespoons raisins
- 2 heaped tablespoons sultanas
- 15 chopped dried apricots

Use as required with fresh fruit, honey or brown sugar and milk.

Luxury Muesli Base ♡♡♡♡

1 heaped tablespoon each of the following:

wheat bran (optional)
chopped hazelnuts
chopped cashews
ground almonds
raisins
chopped dried apricots
sunflower seeds
sesame seeds
6 heaped tablespoons porridge oats

Mix all ingredients together in a bowl and transfer to a storage jar. Use as required. Put 1–2 heaped tablespoons into a cereal bowl. Add brown sugar or honey to taste and fresh fruit, then milk to moisten. For a really special muesli also add 1 tablespoon single cream.

NOTE: There has been some controversy over the real value of muesli in the diet. With commercial products of every sort there is often a leaning towards 'junk' quality and a disregard for nutritional value. Muesli is no exception. At home the situation is quite different, and the best-quality ingredients can be used in the correct proportions to produce a well balanced food. Some people will find muesli more digestible if the oats are soaked in water or milk for a few hours. Put in the fridge overnight, covered, and add the remaining ingredients next morning.

Toasted Muesli (1 serving) ♡♡♡♡

This do-it-yourself cereal is crisper and lower in fat than granola (see p. 38). It is elegant enough to serve in a glass dish for a special breakfast and will tempt the most entrenched muesli hater.

6 quartered hazelnuts
1 tablespoon chopped cashews
½ tablespoon sunflower seeds
1 heaped tablespoon porridge oats
1 scant tablespoon demerara sugar
1 ripe eating-apple
2 chopped dried apricot halves
½ tablespoon sultanas
skimmed milk to serve

Method: Sprinkle the base of a sponge tin evenly with the nuts, seeds, oats and sugar. Put under a hot grill for a minute. Stir with a spoon and continue under the grill for another minute. When it turns golden brown put aside to cool while you peel, core and slice the apple thinly. Put into a bowl and sprinkle with the dried fruit. Pour over a little milk and top with the toasted mixture. Serve immediately.

NOTE: The toasting doesn't take long; just like toasted bread, it only takes a few seconds to overcook and burn, so it needs careful attention. Purists will leave the skin on the apple.

Hot Muesli (1 large or 2 small servings) ♡♡♡♡

There are some winter mornings when a cold breakfast such as muesli seems inappropriate. Here's a hot version to enjoy when it is freezing cold, to give a good warm start to the day.

Base

½ cooking-apple, peeled and cored
water
1 tablespoon sultanas or seedless raisins
demerara sugar or runny honey to taste

Topping

2 heaped tablespoons porridge oats
½ level tablespoon sunflower seeds
1 level tablespoon almonds, cashews or hazelnuts, chopped
1 level tablespoon demerara sugar

Method: Cut the prepared apple into thin slices. Put into a small saucepan with 2 tablespoons of water, dried fruit and sweetening to taste. Set over a gentle heat to cook, stirring from time to time, while you make the topping. Sprinkle the oats, seeds, nuts and sugar into a sponge tin. Mix and spread out to cover the tin. Put under a medium grill for a minute. Turn the tin round and stir the topping. Put back under the grill for another minute and repeat. After 4–5 minutes the crisp topping will be toasted golden brown. Switch off the grill but leave the tin under it. Stir the apple and put into a warmed serving bowl. Spoon the hot topping over the fruit and serve with a heaped tablespoon of plain yoghurt or a tablespoon of single cream. Serve immediately.

NOTE: Keep a careful eye on the topping as it toasts—don't let it brown too much.

Granola (2 servings) ♡♡♡

A crunchy cereal to make at home that can be served warm or cold. Definitely not for slimmers!

2 scant tablespoons sunflower oil
4 heaped tablespoons porridge oats
2 tablespoons chopped mixed nuts (without peanuts)
2 heaped teaspoons wheatgerm
1 heaped tablespoon sunflower seeds
1 heaped tablespoon brown sugar
2 heaped tablespoons sultanas

Method: Put the oats and oil into a heavy-based saucepan. Set over a gentle heat and stir until the oats have absorbed the oil. Sprinkle in the nuts, wheatgerm, seeds and sugar. Continue to heat gently for 10 minutes while you stir. Turn up the heat, still stirring, until it has turned golden brown. Take off the heat, and mix in the sultanas. Serve warm with warm skimmed milk, or cold with cold skimmed milk from the fridge.

Muesli Scones (makes 6) ♡♡♡

Eat this subtly flavoured scone for breakfast, elevenses, tea or as a snack.

½ small banana
4oz (100g) plain flour, wholewheat or unbleached white
2½ level teaspoons baking powder
pinch salt
2oz (50g) polyunsaturated margarine
1oz (25g) soft brown sugar
1 slightly heaped tablespoon sultanas
1 heaped tablespoon porridge oats
1 level tablespoon chopped nuts (avoid peanuts)
2½oz (75ml) milk to mix
milk or runny honey for glaze
porridge oats for sprinkling (optional)

Preheat oven: Gas 7/425°F/220°C/fan oven 200°C
Position: top shelf
Baking time: about 15 minutes/fan oven 10 minutes

Method: Chop the banana into small pieces and put to one side. Mix the flour, baking powder and salt in a bowl. Add the margarine and rub in with the fingers until the mixture resembles breadcrumbs. Sprinkle in the sugar, sultanas, oats, nuts and banana. Stir with a knife until evenly distributed. Make a well in the centre and pour in the milk. Mix by hand to a soft dough, using more flour if too wet. Grease and flour a baking sheet. Put the dough into the centre and lightly press and pat it flat into a round ¾in (2cm) thick. Brush the top with milk or warmed runny honey. Cut in half with a sharp knife, then cut each piece into 3 wedges. Carefully pull them apart, sprinkle with oats (optional) and bake. Cool on a wire rack and serve split and buttered. Eat freshly baked, or toasted the following day.

Breakfast Oat Muffins (makes 6) ♡♡♡

American muffins are completely different from English ones. They both look rather like outsize fairy-cakes with a cracked top, but there are similarity ends. The English sort are a kind of unyeasted soft bread containing fruit, and remarkably low in fat and sugar. Both fresh and dried fruit can be used, to give a wide variety of flavours. They only take a few minutes to make, and are meant to be eaten freshly baked, still warm from the oven.

1½ (40g) porridge oats
3½oz (90g) plain flour, wholewheat or unbleached white
1½ level teaspoons baking powder
pinch salt
1½oz (40g) soft brown sugar
1 large egg
5oz (150ml) milk
2 tablespoons sunflower oil
2½oz (65g) fruit (fresh or dried—*see below*)
grated rind of ¼ lemon (optional)

Preheat oven: Gas 6/400°F/200°C/fan oven 180°C

Position: Top shelf
Baking time: 20–30 minutes/fan oven 14–16 minutes

Method: Grind the oats to flour in a coffee grinder. Put into a bowl with the plain flour, baking powder, salt and sugar. Whisk the egg in a basin. Add the milk and oil. Whisk again. Mix (don't beat) into the dry ingredients. Stir in the fruit of your choice (and the lemon rind, if you are using it). You should now have a sloppy mixture, more like a thick batter than a cake mix. Spoon into a muffin tin lined with 6 papers. Bake. Test one muffin with a skewer. If it comes out clean the muffins are done. Leave in the tin for a minute or two, then turn out on to a wire rack to cool. Serve still warm, for breakfast or brunch.

NOTE: Don't use an electric beater—in fact, don't beat at all, as it will make the muffins tough. Muffin tins are larger and deeper than patty tins, likewise the papers to fit them. They are available from kitchen shops, department stores and iron-mongers.

Fresh fruit options	*Dried fruit options*
eating-apple, chopped	dried apricots, chopped
apricots, stoned and chopped	stoned dates, chopped
banana, chopped	dried peaches, chopped
blackberries	stoned prunes, chopped
blueberries	seedless raisins
cherries, stoned and chopped	sultanas
peaches, stoned and chopped	
eating-pear chopped	
raspberries, quartered	

The fruit should be ripe and sweet. Peel as necessary.

Flying Starts (makes 10 breakfast cookies) ♡♡♡

Not everyone has time to sit down to a proper breakfast in the mornings. Here are some semi-sweet cookies with fruit, nuts and seeds etc. that will fortify breakfast-on-the-hoof people. Wrapped in food film, these cookies slip easily into pocket, bag, lunchbox or briefcase for eating at the earliest opportunity.

A good munch for breakfast, elevenses, brunch or afternoon break, they are also a nourishing food. Two with an apple and a hot drink are quite substantial.

2oz (50g) porridge oats
4oz (100g) plan flour, wholewheat or unbleached white
1 level teaspoon baking powder
2½ (65g) polyunsaturated margarine
1oz (25g) soft brown sugar
1oz (25g) ground nuts (almonds, hazelnuts or cashews)
5oz (135g) fruit (*see below*)
1 tablespoon sunflower seeds
rind of 1 lemon or 1 orange, finely grated
1 egg, beaten
milk to mix, if needed
sesame seeds for finishing

Preheat oven: Gas 5/375°F/190°C/fan oven 170°C
Position: above centre shelf
Baking time: about 20 minutes/fan oven about 14 minutes

Method: Make the oats into flour, using a coffee grinder. Put into a bowl with the plain flour and the baking powder. Mix well by hand. Add the margarine and rub in with the fingertips until the mixture resembles coarse breadcrumbs. Sprinkle in the sugar, nuts, fruit, seeds and rind. Use a knife to stir until all the ingredients are evenly distributed. Pour in the egg and stir again, adding a little milk if necessary to make a stiff mixture. Have ready a greased and floured baking sheet. Spoon into 10 heaps, leaving enough space for them to spread. Flatten out with the back of a metal spoon and sprinkle with sesame seeds. Bake until golden brown, then cool on a wire rack. When they are completely cold, individually wrap the cookies in food film. Store in an airtight container.

Fruit
Use two or more of the following (total weight of the fruit mixture should be 5oz (130g):

fresh eating-apple, chopped into small pieces
dried apricots, chopped
peaches, chopped

pears, chopped
prunes, stoned and chopped
sultanas
seedless raisins

NOTE: Take care not to overbake the cookies, or they will be dry.

Oat Pancakes (makes 5 or 6) ♡♡♡

Fresh or stewed fruit can be used to fill these light pancakes, adding variety to breakfasts all year round.

2oz (50g) porridge oats	1 egg
2oz (50g) plain flour	1 tablespoon sunflower oil
1 teaspoon caster sugar	½pt (300ml) skimmed milk
small pinch salt	

Method: Make the oats into flour, using a coffee grinder. Put into a basin with the plain flour, sugar and salt. Mix well. In a separate basin beat the egg, milk and oil with a fork. Stir in the oat/flour mixture. Beat to a smooth cream, getting out any lumps. Oil a frying pan. Heat until the oil begins to smoke. Pour in about ⅙ of the batter, tipping the pan to allow it to spread evenly over the base. Cook until it bubbles. Loosen with a spatula and turn over (or toss) to cook quickly on the other side. Slide on to a warmed plate and keep warm in a low oven while you make the rest. Have your filling ready (see below). Spread 2 tablespoons over each pancake and roll up. Transfer to warm plates to serve, sprinkled with caster sugar.

Fillings

Apple—use stewed cooking-apple sweetened with caster or demerara sugar
Apple and summerfruits—use cooking-apple stewed with frozen summerfruits: sweeten to taste with caster sugar
Apricots—stone and chop fresh, ripe apricots, stew in a little water, and sweeten to taste with caster or demerara sugar

Blueberries—chop small, saving the juice, then sweeten with caster sugar if necessary (allow 1 heaped tablespoon of berries per pancake)
Lemon—use ½ a lemon for 2 pancakes: squeeze the lemon over each pancake, sprinkle with caster sugar and roll up
Orange—use 1 orange for 3 pancakes: squeeze orange halves over each pancake, sprinkle with caster sugar and roll up
Peaches—use ripe, sweet fruit: cut out the stones, peel and chop the flesh on a board, then sweeten to taste with caster or demerara sugar
Raspberries—mash 1 heaped tablespoon per pancake, then sweeten to taste with caster sugar
Rhubarb and apple—stew rhubarb with cooking-apples and a squeeze of fresh lemon juice, then sweeten to taste with caster sugar
Strawberries—hull and chop very small or mash, allowing 3–4 strawberries per pancake, then sweeten to taste with caster sugar

NOTE: Keep a saucer of sunflower oil by you when you make these. Dip into it with a screw of kitchen paper and oil the pan before making each pancake, while the pan is off the heat.

Skinless Pork and Oat Sausages (makes 12 medium-sized, or 20 small) ♡♡♡
Make the night before, for breakfast. Put the sausages on a plate dusted with flour and cover with food film. Store overnight in the fridge.

- 1oz (25g) porridge oats
- about 6oz (170g) raw lean pork
- 1 medium cooking-apple, finely grated
- 1oz (25g) fresh breadcrumbs
- 1 tablespoon soy sauce
- 1 tablespoon sunflower oil
- 2 good pinches allspice
- 2 good pinches dried mixed herbs, or 4 pinches fresh chopped
- salt and freshly ground black pepper
- plain flour for coating
- sunflower oil for frying

Method: Grind the oats to flour in a coffee grinder. Trim off and discard all fat and gristle from the pork. Cut the lean into small pieces and either put through a mincer or process in a food processor. Put the prepared meat into a basin with the oat flour, grated apple, breadcrumbs, soy sauce, oil, spices, herbs and seasoning to taste. Mix by hand to a sticky paste. Put a handful of flour on to a plate. Put 1 heaped tablespoon of the paste on to the plate and shape into a sausage, turning it over to coat it. Continue until you have used up all the paste. Fry in hot shallow oil for 5 or 6 minutes, turning them over after 3 minutes. When brown, crisp and cooked right through serve with hot canned tomatoes.

NOTE: These sausages can be frozen for later use. Leave raw and wrap individually before putting into the freezer. Thaw slowly for several hours before frying.

CHAPTER 4

Soups, Starters and Main Courses

Asparagus Soup with Oats (serves 3 or 4) ♡♡♡♡

This soup avoids the traditional addition of cream and so is lighter and has a more delicate flavour. However, it still retains its smooth, creamy texture. With its pretty pale-green colour, always an impressive soup to serve at a dinner or lunch party. Buy organic asparagus if available, as it has the best taste.

1 heaped teaspoon polyunsaturated margarine
¼ medium onion, finely chopped
15fl oz (450ml) water
1 tablespoon porridge oats
½ teaspoon low-fat dried milk granules
3 teaspoons soy sauce
1 × 250g bundle fresh asparagus
salt and freshly ground black pepper

Method: Melt the margarine in a medium saucepan over a gentle heat. Put in the onion and stir/fry for 3 or 4 minutes, but don't let it brown. Pour in the water, add the oats, milk granules and soy sauce. Stir and bring to the boil. Have ready the asparagus with ⅕ trimmed off the bottoms of the stalks and discarded. Cut off the tips and put to one side. Cut the stalks into short lengths and put into the saucepan. Bring back to the boil, then reduce the heat and let it simmer for 5 minutes. Put in the tips, bring back to the boil and reduce the heat to simmer again for another 5 minutes. Cool for 5 minutes, then pour into a liquidiser goblet and blend. Pour back into the saucepan. Season to taste and serve hot with brown bread and butter.

NOTE: Don't be put off by the strange combination of asparagus and oats.

Leek and Oatmeal Soup (5 or 6 servings) ♡♡♡♡

This is a velvety-smooth, creamy soup although no cream is used to make it. A heart-warming dish for cold wintry days.

1 tablespoon sunflower oil
½ medium onion, finely chopped
2 medium-sized leeks, trimmed and sliced
1½pt (900ml) water
2 tablespoons porridge oats
1 slightly heaped tablespoon low-fat dried milk granules
1 tablespoon soy sauce
salt and freshly ground black pepper
small slice of tender green leek, finely chopped for garnish

Method: Using a large saucepan, gently fry the onion in the oil for 3 or 4 minutes, but don't let it brown. Add the leeks and stir/fry for 1 minute. Pour in the water, sprinkle in the oats and milk granules and add the soy sauce. Stir well and bring to the boil. Reduce heat to a simmer for 15–20 minutes, until the leeks are tender. Leave to cool for a few minutes, then pour into a blender goblet. Strain some of the liquid back into the saucepan, as the blending process with this soup is rather splashy. Blend what is left in the goblet, and pour it back into the saucepan. Heat through and season to taste. Serve in bowls, with a sprinkle of the garnish in the centre.

Chicken, Oat and Vegetable Soup (4 servings) ♡♡♡♡

A creamy, golden farmhouse soup—a meal in itself. The oats will thicken the soup to perfection during the cooking.

½ medium onion, thinly sliced
1 tablespoon sunflower oil
1pt (600ml) water
½ medium carrot, thinly sliced
1 chopped stick celery
3 teaspoons soy sauce
1 heaped tablespoon porridge oats
1 teaspoon low-fat dried milk granules
2 level tablespoons chopped fresh parsley
4 heaped tablespoons chopped cooked chicken meat
1 teaspoon fresh lemon juice
salt and freshly ground black pepper

Method: Use a medium-sized saucepan to gently fry the onion in the oil for 3 or 4 minutes, stirring from time to time. Add the water, carrot, celery, soy sauce and oats. Stir in the dried milk. Add half the parsley and half the chicken pieces. Stir again and bring to the boil. Reduce the heat and simmer for 15 minutes. Strain into a basin. Put half the liquid and all of the solid pieces into a liquidiser. Blend and return to the saucepan with the rest of the strained liquid. Add the lemon juice and the remaining chicken meat. Bring back to the boil and simmer for 3 minutes. Stir in the rest of the parsley and season to taste. Serve hot with crusty bread or rolls.

Herrings in Oatmeal (2 servings) ♡♡♡♡

A traditional dish eaten for supper, high tea or even breakfast. For a simple main meal serve with a green side salad and follow with fresh fruit.

2 small herrings, prepared (see note below)
salt and freshly ground black pepper
about ½ teacup milk
2 level teaspoons pinhead (coarse) oatmeal
1½oz (40g) polyunsaturated margarine
lemon quarters to garnish

Method: Open the fish up and sprinkle with salt and pepper. Pour the milk into a shallow bowl. Close up the fish and dip them in the milk. Have the oatmeal ready on a plate. Press the fish firmly on to the plate so the oatmeal will coat them, both sides. Melt the margarine in a heavy-based pan. Fry the fish over a gentle heat for 10 minutes, then turn over carefully with a fish slice to cook on the other side for a further 10 minutes. Lift the fish on to warmed plates and spoon over a little of the margarine from the pan. Garnish with the lemon wedges and serve with brown bread rolls.

NOTE: Herrings can be bought ready-prepared from supermarkets and fishmongers. They should be scaled, washed and cleaned, with heads cut off and backbones removed.

Trout in Oatmeal ♡♡♡♡

Make as for herrings in oatmeal, substituting small trout for the herrings.

Whitebait in Oatflour (serves 2) ♡♡♡♡

These tiny fish are the fry of herring. Although herrings are traditionally fried in oatmeal, this would be out of scale for such small fish.

Method: Grind about 1oz (25g) porridge oats to flour in a coffee grinder. Put into a plastic bag with a good pinch of salt. Wash about 4oz (100g) whitebait and pat dry with kitchen paper. Put about 6 at a time into the bag, hold it closed and shake to coat the fish. Fry in hot shallow oil, turning once, for 1 or 2 minutes each side depending on how tiny they are. Drain on kitchen paper and serve on warm tea-plates with a wedge of lemon and thin slices of brown bread and butter. A traditional starter, but can also be served for high tea or supper.

NOTE: The heat should be fairly high to crisp the oat flour and turn it golden brown. The fish themselves will be cooked in a few seconds.

SAVOURY OAT PANCAKES ♡♡♡

Make the pancake recipe on p. 42 but omit sugar. The fillings should be put hot into the pancakes.

Basic White Sauce

- 1 heaped tablespoon dried milk granules (low fat)
- 2 slightly heaped teaspoons cornflour
- ¼ pint (150ml) cold water

Method: Mix the dried milk into the water in a small saucepan (preferably a non-stick, heavy-based one). Put the cornflour into a jug and add scant 2 tablespoons of the milk. Stir until smooth then add to the saucepan. Heat gently while you stir. When almost at boiling point, reduce the heat and continue stirring for another minute until thickened.

Cheese Sauce

Make basic white sauce and take off the heat. Stir in ½ teaspoon made French mustard and add 1 level tablespoon finely grated tasty cheddar cheese. Stir until the cheese has melted in.

Mushroom Pancake

Cook chopped mushrooms in a little polyunsaturated margarine, a touch of crushed garlic, salt and pepper to taste, and either a little cheese sauce or single cream. Two tablespoons of the mixture are enough to fill one pancake. Garnish with parsley.

Leek and Cheese Pancake

Simmer sliced leeks in boiling water until tender. Drain, pressing with the back of a spoon while still in the colander. Stir into cheese sauce. Use 1 heaped tablespoon per pancake, roll up, and serve sprinkled with finely grated Parmesan cheese.

Chicken Pancake

Use 1 tablespoon chopped cooked lean chicken meat per pancake. Stir into white sauce and add a squeeze of lemon and a sprinkle of chopped fresh parsley. Garnish with parsley.

Fresh Salmon Pancake

Make as for chicken but use fresh poached salmon, flaked or mashed. Garnish with lemon twists and sprigs of parsley.

Prawn Pancake

Mix defrosted peeled prawns into a white sauce to which has been added a squeeze of lemon. For one pancake, allow 2 tablespoons of white sauce to 8 prawns. Garnish with a sprig of parsley and a twist of lemon.

NOTE: Per pancake, allow 2–3 tablespoons of white or cheese sauce as a base for each kind of filling.

Oat Sausages (makes 4) ♡♡♡♡

The ideal vegetarian sausage for everyone, as good cold as hot.

- 2 heaped tablespoons rolled oats
- 2 heaped tablespoons onion, finely chopped
- 2 heaped tablespoons cooked butter-beans, mashed (see note below)
- 3 good pinches mixed dried herbs
- 1 tablespoon sunflower oil
- salt and freshly ground black pepper
- 4 tablespoons cold water
- plain flour for rolling
- sunflower oil for frying

Method: Make the oats into flour, using a coffee grinder. Put into a basin with the onion, mashed beans, herbs and oil. Season with salt and pepper to taste and add the water. With a fork, mix to a stiff paste. Put a little flour on a saucer. Divide the mixture into four and shape each piece into a sausage. Roll in the flour and fry in hot, shallow oil for about 6 minutes, turning frequently. When crisp and golden brown, drain on kitchen paper. Serve hot with potatoes or rice, vegetables and gravy, or cold with salad and bread. For party nibbles, cut each hot, cooked sausage into 5 pieces and put a cocktail stick into each one. Serve on a warm plate.

Variations

- Use baked beans (rinsed in a sieve) instead of butter beans.
- Add ¼ teaspoon garlic put through a garlic crusher.
- After rolling in flour, dip in beaten egg and roll in breadcrumbs before shallow-frying.
- Use the uncooked sausages to make sausage rolls.

NOTE: Use drained canned butter-beans.

Vegetarian Oat Rissoles (makes 8 medium-sized) ♡♡♡

No-nonsense meat replacer for the vegetarian or vegan. Tasty, filling and easy to make.

1 tablespoon sunflower oil
1 medium onion, finely sliced
1 heaped tablespoon mushrooms, finely chopped
2oz (50g) wholewheat breadcrumbs
2oz (50g) porridge oats
1 tablespoon soy sauce
1 heaped teaspoon tomato purée
6oz (170g) ground mixed nuts
¼ level teaspoon dried mixed herbs, or ½ teaspoon freshly chopped
10oz (300ml) hot water
salt and freshly ground black pepper
more porridge oats for coating
sunflower oil for frying

Method: Fry the onion gently in the oil for 3 or 4 minutes, to soften. Add the mushrooms and stir/fry for a minute. Put into a basin with the breadcrumbs, oats, soy sauce, purée, nuts and herbs. Mix well. Add the water and stir, to make a moist mixture. Season to taste. Sprinkle oats on to a plate. Divide the rissole mixture into 8. Shape each portion into a flat cake by hand. Press into the oats on each side and fry in hot shallow oil for 4 minutes. Turn over with a spatula and fry on the other side. Drain on kitchen paper and serve with vegetables and good gravy.

Vegetarian Oat Roast (serves 4) ♡♡♡♡

Make as for vegetarian oat rissoles, but instead of shaping the mixture into rissoles turn it into a greased shallow ovenproof dish. Flatten the surface with a knife and sprinkle the top with oats. Bake in a preheated oven at Gas 4/350°F/180°C/fan oven 160°C on the top shelf for 30 minutes/fan oven 20 minutes. To serve, cut into slices. Serve hot with vegetables and gravy, or cold with salad.

Vegetarian Cottage Pie with Oats (serves 4) ♡♡♡

Make the base with the vegetarian oat rissole mixture, but use 2 heaped tablespoons finely chopped mushrooms and enough extra hot water to make a wetter mixture. Put into an ovenproof casserole and cover the top with a layer of mashed potato (see below). Use a fork to texture it. Bake at Gas 6/400°F/200°C/ fan oven 180°C for about 30 minutes/fan oven 20 minutes above the centre shelf, until the potato is crisp and golden brown. Serve hot with vegetables.

Mashed Potato

Peel and thickly slice 1½lb (700g) old potatoes. Boil in salted water for 15 minutes or so until soft. Drain and mash with a potato masher, adding a knob of polyunsaturated margarine and salt and freshly ground black pepper to taste, plus 2 good pinches of ground nutmeg. Beat with a wooden spoon to make it smooth.

Vegetable and Oat Rissoles (makes 4) ♡♡♡♡

A vegetarian dish that can be made ahead.

3oz (75g) cooked beans, mashed (see note below)
½ medium onion, finely chopped
½ stalk celery, finely chopped
½ medium carrot, grated
1oz (25g) cooked green beans, finely chopped
1oz (25g) porridge oats
1½ eggs, beaten
2 pinches salt
4 grinds black pepper
½ beaten egg for coating
porridge oats for rolling
sunflower oil for frying

Method: Put the mashed beans into a bowl with the remaining ingredients. Mix until thoroughly combined. Put to one side for at least 20 minutes to firm up. Divide into 4. With floured hands, shape into balls, then flatten between the palms to make cakes. Brush on both sides with the egg and roll in the oats on a plate. Fry in hot, shallow oil over a medium heat for 10 minutes on each side until golden brown. Drain on kitchen paper and serve hot with suitable gravy and rice or potatoes.

NOTE: For the beans use canned baked beans, haricot beans or red kidney beans. Put into a wire sieve and rinse under the tap before mashing.

Oat Pasta (makes 5½oz (155g) fresh) ♡♡♡♡

Cooked pasta should be *al dente* (firm to the bite). This is easily achieved with oat pasta. Its only drawback is its rather dreary oatmeal colour. However, it can be cheered up with a rich red sauce and a sprinkle of Parmesan cheese.

1oz (25g) porridge oats
2½oz (65g) strong white flour
1 pinch salt
1 egg
2 teaspoons sunflower oil

Method: Grind the oats to flour using a coffee grinder. Put into a bowl with the strong white flour and the salt. Mix and make a well in the centre. Break the egg into a cup and add the oil. Whisk with a fork and pour into the well. Stir the egg mixture, gradually pulling in the flour to make a stiff dough. Knead in the bowl for 1 minute, then on a lightly floured worktop for another 2 minutes, until the dough feels smooth and elastic. Leave to rest in the bowl for 20–30 minutes. Cut in half. Roll out one of the pieces on a floured worktop. Keep turning it round and rolling—the pasta will grow larger and larger—until it is as thin as paper. Repeat with the second piece of dough. Cut into strips for tagliatelle using a pasta wheel (the zigzag kind). Use for ravioli, lasagne etc. in place of ordinary wheatflour pasta.

NOTE: Resting the dough produces a better pasta. However, if you don't have the time to wait, proceed straight to rolling out.

To cook
Have ready a large saucepan of boiling salted water. Drop in the pasta by the handful, bring back to the boil and cook for 4–5 minutes. Drain in a colander, then put the pasta back into the saucepan. Add a knob of polyunsaturated margarine and stir carefully to coat, but try not to damage the pasta. Serve immediately.

Crunchy Oat Coating for Fish (enough for 2 fillets, or 20 goujons) ♡♡♡

Fish Fillets

2oz (50g) porridge oats
¼ teaspoon dry mustard powder
2 fillets cod or haddock
plain flour for dusting
1 egg, beaten on a plate
lemon quarters and sprigs of parsley for garnish
sunflower oil for frying

Method: Mix the oats with the mustard and put on to a plate. Wash the fish fillets and pat dry with kitchen paper. Dust all over with flour. Dip them in the egg, making sure both sides are coated. Roll in the oat mixture. Fry in hot shallow oil, turning once until the fish is tender and the coating golden. Drain on kitchen paper and serve immediately with vegetables, garnished with a lemon quarter and parsley.

Goujons (fish strips) ♡♡♡
Use the same recipe ingredients for the coating as for fish fillets above. Wash plaice fillets, pat dry with kitchen paper, cut into strips and dust with the flour. Dip in the beaten egg. Have the oat coating ready in a plastic bag. Put the prepared fish strips into the bag, five at a time. Holding the top closed, shake to coat. Fry in the hot shallow oil, turning once. Drain

on kitchen paper. If served as nibbles, put them on to a warm plate with a small bowl of dipping sauce and cocktail sticks. As a starter, serve on warm plates with lemon wedges and parsley. Alternatively, use sauce tartare instead of the lemon. Brown bread and butter is the traditional accompaniment.

Fish Crumble with Oats (serves 2) ♡♡♡

Colour and texture are not the strong points of white fish—in fact, it can be positively uninspiring. In this recipe, the colour is enlivened by the tomato and egg, and the oat topping provides an interesting texture to contrast with the soft base.

Base

- ¼pt (150ml) milk
- 1 small bayleaf
- 1 tablespoon chopped fresh parsley
- 8oz (225g) cod or haddock, skinned and boned
- 1 fresh tomato, peeled and sliced
- 1 hard-boiled egg, chopped
- 1oz (25g) polyunsaturated margarine
- white of 4 spring onions, finely chopped
- ½oz (15g) plain flour
- 1 level teaspoon made French mustard
- salt and freshly ground black pepper

Topping

- 1½oz (40g) plain flour
- 1oz (25g) porridge oats
- 1oz (25g) polyunsaturated margarine

Preheat oven: Gas 5/375°F/190°C/fan oven 170°C
Position: above centre shelf
Baking time: about 20 minutes/fan oven about 14 minutes

Method: Put the milk, bayleaf and parsley into a small saucepan with the fish. Poach for a few minutes. When cooked, discard the bayleaf and strain the fish, saving the poaching liquid. Grease an ovenproof dish. Cover the base with the tomato slices. Sprinkle with the chopped egg and place the poached fish on top. Now make the topping. Mix the flour and oats in a basin. Rub in the margarine until the mixture resembles coarse breadcrumbs.

Continue with the base. Melt the margarine in a small saucepan. Sprinkle in the onion and stir/cook over a gentle heat for 2 minutes. Mix in the flour. Take off the heat and gradually stir in the poaching liquid, beating out any lumps. Add the mustard and return to the heat. Bring to the boil, stirring. Cook for 2 minutes. Season the fish to taste and pour the sauce over. Sprinkle evenly with the prepared topping and bake until crisp and golden. Serve immediately with peas and carrots, broccoli or spinach, for a tasty main course.

British-style Oat Pizza (makes 1 large or 2 small, or 4 starter-size) ♡♡♡

Italian-style pizza features oil in the dough, on the pizza and over it, as well as Italian plum tomatoes, Parmesan cheese, and vegetables and herbs from sunnier climes such as basil and olives. Oats have been added to this pizza dough that follows, so more appropriate toppings can be made from British ingredients—leeks, onions, potatoes, rosemary, parsley, bacon, ham, mushrooms, tasty Cheddar cheese and British tomatoes, which have quite a different flavour and texture from plum tomatoes. Too much fat is avoided, so it is easier to digest and altogether healthier.

Dough

1oz (25g) porridge oats
¼oz (7g) instant 'fast action' yeast
3oz (75g) strong flour
pinch salt
2 pinches sugar
1 tablespoon sunflower oil
1 tablespoon warm water

Basic topping

4 medium tomatoes, sliced
4 pinches caster sugar
freshly ground black pepper
2 heaped tablespoons tasty Cheddar cheese, finely grated

Preheat oven: Gas 7/425°F/220°C/fan oven 200°C
Position: top shelf
Baking time: 15–20 minutes/fan oven 10–12 minutes

Method: Make the oats into flour, using a coffee grinder. Put into a bowl with the yeast, plain flour, salt and sugar. Mix well, then drizzle in the oil. Add the water and mix to a soft dough. Put it on to a floured worktop, then pick it up and slap it down hard. Turn the dough over and repeat twice more. Knead for a minute until smooth, then flour the worktop again and roll out thinly into a circle. Lay the rolling-pin halfway across it, loop half the dough over it and lift it on to a greased baking sheet. Turn the edge over all the way round, like a hem (this will contain all the filling).

Now arrange the slices of tomato to cover the base. Sprinkle with the sugar. Season with the pepper, then cover with the grated cheese. Leave to rise in a warm place for about 10 minutes. Bake. Cut into portions on the baking sheet and serve on warm plates with a knife and fork.

NOTE: Pizza makes a good nibble to eat with drinks. Bake and cut into small pieces. Serve on a paper serviette laid on a warm plate.

Leek and Potato Pizza ♡♡♡♡

½ medium leek, thinly sliced
½ medium potato, sliced
4 medium tomatoes, thinly sliced
4 pinches caster sugar
freshly ground black pepper
2 heaped tablespoons tasty Cheddar cheese, finely grated

Method: Cook the leek and potato in boiling water. Simmer for 10 minutes, then strain. Chop the potato into small pieces. Arrange the tomato slices on the pizza base and sprinkle with the sugar. Distribute the leek and potato over the tomatoes and season with pepper to taste. Top with the cheese. Leave in a warm place to rise for 10 minutes, then bake.

Using the same dough for the base, try these:

Ham and Mushroom Pizza ♡♡♡♡

- 4 medium tomatoes, thinly sliced
- 4 pinches caster sugar
- 2 slices lean ham, cut into small squares
- 3–4 medium mushrooms, chopped small
- 1 level tablespoon chopped fresh parsley
- freshly ground black pepper
- 2 heaped tablespoons tasty Cheddar cheese, finely grated

Method: Arrange the tomato slices on the pizza base. Sprinkle with the sugar. Cover with the ham and mushrooms. Season with black pepper and sprinkle the cheese over. Leave to rise in a warm place for 10 minutes, then bake. Scatter the parsley over before serving.

Onion, Bacon and Rosemary Pizza ♡♡♡♡

- 4 medium tomatoes, thinly sliced
- 1 medium onion, thinly sliced
- 2 rashers lean back bacon, trimmed of fat, grilled
- 1 teaspoon chopped fresh rosemary, or ½ teaspoon dried
- freshly ground black pepper
- 2 heaped tablespoons tasty Cheddar cheese, finely grated

Method: Arrange the tomato slices over the pizza base. Cover with the sliced onion. Chop the bacon into small pieces, and scatter it over the onion. Sprinkle with the rosemary. Season with black pepper and top with the cheese. Leave to rise in a warm place for 10 minutes, then bake.

NOTE: The onions will be slightly sweet, and so sugar is not required for the tomatoes.

SAVOURY CAKES OR RISSOLES WITH OAT COATING

Cooked fish or meat, chopped or ground nuts or grated cheese can be mixed with mashed potato and herbs and formed into flat cakes, then coated in plain flour, egg and porridge oats and fried in shallow oil to make the protein part of a main meal. Leftovers from a joint or poultry, or canned fish, are equally suitable. The choice of herbs can transform these savoury cakes, and the oat coating provides an interesting texture for what is really a rather humble food. Add a good gravy or sauce and fresh vegetables, and you have a satisfying and nutritious meal that can be made quickly, and varied according to what is available in the way of ingredients.

The method is the same for each kind of rissole: Put the prepared fish/meat/nuts/cheese into a bowl with the mashed potato and prepared herb or herbs, sauces etc. Season to taste with salt and freshly ground black pepper. Mix everything together and with your hands form into flat cakes. Have ready a little plain flour sprinkled on a plate. Dip each cake in the flour on both sides and roll it so that the edges are also coated.

With a fork, whisk an egg on a saucer. Put each savoury cake into the saucer and brush the top with the beaten egg, so that each is coated all over with it. Sprinkle porridge oats or oat flour on to a plate. Press each cake into the oats, turn it over and coat the other side. Fry in hot shallow oil, turning once with a spatula after about 3 minutes, and continuing to fry for another 3 minutes. The cakes should then be crisp and golden, ready to drain on kitchen paper. Serve hot, as described above.

Here are a few suggestions for savoury cakes, each enough to make 2 medium-sized or 3 small cakes (1 serving). (Large cakes are difficult to turn over and inclined to break.) Allow about 3oz (75g) fish/meat etc. per portion.

Fishcakes ♡♡♡♡

1 portion cod or haddock, baked or poached
2 heaped tablespoons mashed potato
1 heaped tablespoon fresh parsley, finely chopped
salt and pepper to taste
½ teaspoon fresh lemon juice
flour, egg and porridge oats for finishing (see above for method).

Serve with tomato sauce.

Tuna Fishcakes ♡♡♡♡

½ medium can tuna, drained and mashed
2 heaped tablespoons mashed potato
1 tablespoon tomato ketchup
1 heaped teaspoon fresh parsley, finely chopped
salt and pepper to taste
flour, egg and porridge oats for finishing (see p. 59 for method).

Serve with tomato sauce.

Sardine Fishcakes ♡♡♡♡

2 canned sardines, drained and mashed
1½ heaped tablespoons mashed potato
½ teaspoon fresh lemon juice
1 heaped teaspoon fresh parsley, finely chopped
1 tablespoon porridge oats
pepper to taste
flour, egg and porridge oats for finishing (see p.59 for method).

Serve with tomato sauce.

Chicken Rissoles ♡♡♡♡

1 portion cooked lean chicken, finely chopped
2 heaped tablespoons mashed potato
small pinch powdered cloves (optional)
½ level teaspoon fresh mixed herbs, finely chopped, or ¼ teaspoon dried
½ teaspoon fresh lemon juice
¼ teaspoon soy sauce
salt and pepper to taste
flour, egg and porridge oats for finishing (see p. 59 for method).

Serve with gravy.

Beef Rissoles ♡♡♡♡

1 portion cooked lean roast beef, minced
2 heaped tablespoons mashed potato
½ teaspoon made mustard or horseradish sauce
½ teaspoon soy sauce
1 level teaspoon fresh parsley, finely chopped
salt and pepper to taste
for finishing (see p.59 for method).

Serve with gravy.

Pork Rissoles ♡♡♡♡

- 1 portion roast lean pork, minced
- 1½ heaped tablespoons mashed potato
- ¼ eating-apple, finely grated
- ½ teaspoon soy sauce
- ½ teaspoon fresh sage, finely chopped, or ¼ teaspoon dried
- salt and pepper to taste
- flour, egg and porridge oats for finishing (see p. 59 for method).

Serve with gravy.

Vegetarian Rissoles ♡♡♡♡

- 1 level teaspoon chopped mixed nuts (no peanuts)
- 1 heaped tablespoon baked beans, mashed
- 2 heaped tablespoons mashed potato
- 1 teaspoon tomato purée
- 1 heaped teaspoon Parmesan cheese, finely grated
- 1 heaped teaspoon chopped fresh parsley
- milk to bind
- salt and pepper to taste
- flour, egg and porridge oats for finishing (see p. 59 for method).

Serve with suitable gravy.

Cheese Rissoles ♡♡♡

- 1 level tablespoon tasty Cheddar cheese, finely grated
- 1 level teaspoon Parmesan cheese, finely grated
- 1½ heaped tablespoons mashed potato
- white of two spring onions, finely chopped
- 1 level teaspoon fresh parsley, finely chopped
- 1 canned tomato, chopped small
- ¼ teaspoon made mustard
- ½ beaten egg
- 1 heaped teaspoon porridge oats
- flour, egg and porridge oats for finishing (see p. 59 for method).

Serve with tomato gravy.

Savoury Pie with Oat Pastry (4 servings) ♡♡♡

A versatile pie to serve hot or cold for a main meal, packed lunch or picnic. Make it with eggs and cheese for vegetarians or with ham for meat eaters.

6oz (170g) oat shortcrust pastry (see recipe on p. 63)
3 medium-sized old potatoes
2 medium leeks
2oz (50g) tasty Cheddar cheese, finely grated
salt and freshly ground black pepper
2 eggs, lightly beaten
porridge oats for finishing

Preheat oven: Gas 7/425°F/220°C/fan oven 200°C
Position: top shelf
Baking time: about 15 minutes/fan oven 10 minutes

Method: Make the pastry and put to one side to rest. Peel the potatoes and cut into ¼in (5mm) thick slices. Prepare the leeks and slice into short lengths. Put into a saucepan with the potatoes and pour over enough boiling water to cover. Bring to the boil and cook steadily for 10 minutes. Strain in a colander. Roll out the pastry. Wet the edge of a deep oval pie dish and line the edge with narrow strips of pastry. Turn the partly cooked vegetables into the dish. Sprinkle the cheese over and season to taste. Pour in most of the egg. Wet the pastry edge liner and put on the pastry lid. Press the edges together to seal them, then press the prongs of a table fork all round the edge. Cut a small hole in the centre and brush the pastry with the remaining egg. Sprinkle with a few porridge oats. (Any remaining egg can be poured into the pie through the central hole.) Bake until golden.

Variation

- Cut 1 slice of ham into small squares. Scatter over the vegetables before you put in the cheese.

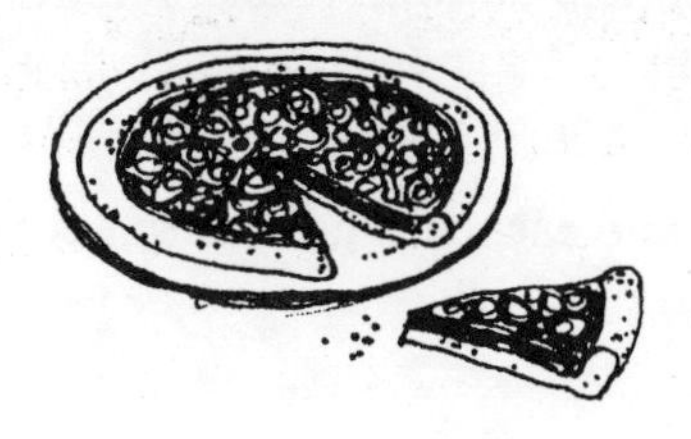

CHAPTER 5

Pastry, Puddings and Desserts

Oat Shortcrust Pastry ♡♡♡

This pastry is crisper and less crumbly than ordinary pastry and easier to handle. It has a subtle 'nutty' flavour that goes well with sweet or savoury dishes. The recipe gives enough pastry (6oz/170g) to line an 8in (20cm) tart tin.

1oz (25g) porridge oats
3oz (75g) plain unbleached white flour
pinch salt
2oz (50g) polyunsaturated margarine
2 tablespoons water
more flour for kneading/rolling out

Method: Grind the oats to flour in a coffee grinder. Put into a bowl with the plain flour and salt. Mix well. Add the margarine and rub in with the fingertips until the mixture resembles fine breadcrumbs. Keep the mixture light by lifting your hands over the bowl and letting the crumbs sprinkle back into it. Spoon in the water and stir with a fork to make the 'crumbs' stick together and leave the bowl clean. Lightly flour the work-top and put the dough on to it. Knead for a few seconds only. If you have the time, leave to rest for 10 minutes or so before rolling out and using.

NOTE: By using unbleached flour a cream-coloured pastry can be produced—ordinary white flour tends to result in a greyish pastry.

Oat Quiche Pastry ♡♡♡

Make as for oat shortcrust pastry, but use self-raising flour instead of plain.

Brown Oat Pastry ♡♡♡♡

Make as for oat shortcrust pastry, but use fine plain wholewheat flour instead of white, and a little more water.

Sweet Oat Shortcrust Pastry ♡♡

Make as for oat shortcrust pastry, but include 1 tablespoon caster sugar and use milk instead of water.

Treacle Tart (makes 6 slices) ♡

One of the great comfort foods. This version uses oats in the pastry as well as in the filling.

- 6oz (170g) oat shortcrust pastry (see recipe on p. 63)
- 4 rounded tablespoons golden syrup
- 4 rounded tablespoons porridge oats
- finely grated rind and juice of ½ lemon

Preheat oven: Gas 6/400°F/200°C/fan oven 180°C
Position: top shelf
Baking time: 25 minutes/fan oven 16 minutes

Method: Roll out the pastry and line an 8in (20cm) tart tin. Trim off all round with a knife, and flute the edge with the fingertips. Warm the syrup gently in a small pan until thin and runny. Stir in the lemon rind and juice. Pour into the pastry case. Sprinkle over the oats as evenly as you can. Roll out the pastry trimmings and cut into strips. Use to make a lattice over the filling. Bake for 10 minutes, then turn down the oven to Gas 5/375°F/190°C/fan oven 170°C and bake for a further 15 minutes. Serve warm or cold for a snack, or as a pudding with custard, single cream, natural yoghurt or a small scoop of vanilla ice-cream.

Date and Oat Tart (makes 8 wedges) ♡♡

As sweet as a treacle tart, but without any sugar added; dark and sticky, with oats in the pastry and in the filling.

5oz (135g) dessert-grade dates
6oz (170g) oat shortcrust pastry (see recipe on p. 63)
about 1 cup water
1 heaped tablespoon porridge oats

Preheat oven: Gas 7/425°F/220°C/fan oven 200°C
Position: top shelf
Baking time: 20–25 minutes/fan oven 14–18 minutes

Method: Cut the dates in half and remove the stones. Chop the flesh and put into a small saucepan with the water. Stir/cook until they have formed a stiff paste. Leave to cool. Roll out the pastry and line a large ovenproof plate. Pinch a raised edge all round with your fingertips. Use a knife to spread the date paste all over the pastry up to the raised edge. Sprinkle with the oats, pressing them slightly into the dates. Bake. Eat hot with custard or a scoop of natural yoghurt as a pudding, or serve cold as a snack.

Oat and Apple Strudel (serves 5-6) ♡♡♡

Crisp and flaky on the outside, with a moist, spicy filling. Serve this strudel for elevenses or tea, or as a pudding with plain yoghurt, custard or single cream. For a dinner party or lunch party serve in small slices, still warm, with a scoop of vanilla ice-cream (there will be enough for 8–9 servings).

Pastry

1oz (25g) porridge oats
2oz (50g) plain flour
½ beaten egg
2 tablespoons sunflower oil
2 tablespoons warm water
more flour for kneading etc.
more oil for brushing

Filling

2 eating-apples
1½oz (40g) sultanas
1 heaped tablespoon caster or soft brown sugar
½ teaspoon cinnamon or mixed spice
1 tablespoon fresh lemon juice
finely grated rind of ½ lemon
½oz (15g) porridge oats

Preheat oven: Gas 7/425°F/220°C/fan oven 200°C
Position: above centre shelf
Baking time: about 40 minutes/fan oven about 25 minutes

Method: Make the 1oz (25g) oats into flour using a coffee grinder. Put into a bowl with the plain flour and mix well. Use a fork to whisk the beaten egg, 2 tablespoons oil and the warm water. Make a well in the flour mixture and pour in the liquid. Mix to a soft dough. Turn out on to a floured worktop and knead for 2 or 3 minutes, until it feels smooth. Put back into the bowl to rest for about half an hour.

Preheat the oven while you make the filling. Peel and core the apples, then grate coarsely and put into a bowl with the sultanas, sugar, spice, lemon juice and rind. Mix with a fork. Now place a large sheet of greaseproof paper on the worktop and dust with flour. Put the pastry in the centre and roll it out, using more flour until it is as thin as paper. Brush with oil, leaving a ½in (1cm) unoiled margin all round. Grind the ½oz (15g) porridge oats to a flour in a coffee grinder. Sprinkle over the oiled pastry. Wet the unoiled margin with cold water, all round. Spread the filling over the oat flour. Lifting one end of the greaseproof paper so as to make the pastry fold over, roll it all up, as shown. Keep lifting the paper to continue the roll. When completely rolled up, pinch all along the edge and the

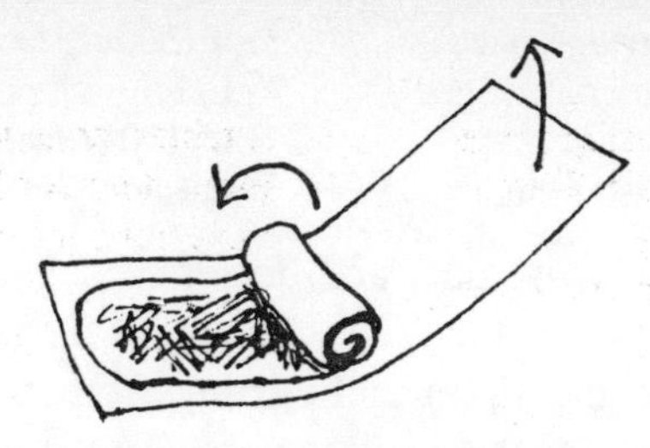

ends to seal. Lift on to a greased baking sheet, arranging the strudel diagonally. Brush with oil and bake. Leave to cool while still on the baking sheet. Dust with icing sugar, and serve cut into lengths or slices.

Oat and Almond Tarts (makes 12) ♡♡♡

A treat for tea or elevenses, dainty little tarts with oats in the pastry and in the almond filling.

6oz (170g) oat shortcrust pastry (see recipe on p. 63)
raspberry jam
½oz (15g) porridge oats
2oz (50g) caster sugar
2oz (50g) ground almonds
few drops almond flavouring
1 large egg, beaten
flaked almonds for finishing

Preheat oven: Gas 6/400°F/200°C/fan oven 180°C
Position: top shelf
Baking time: about 12 minutes/fan oven 8 minutes

Method: Roll out the pastry and line 12 patty tins. Spread ½ teaspoon of jam in the bottom of each one. Grind the oats to flour, using a coffee grinder. Put into a basin with the sugar and ground almonds and flavouring. Mix well. Add the egg and beat well for a minute until smooth and creamy. Using a teaspoon, fill the tartlets with the mixture. Sprinkle with the flaked almonds and bake until golden. Eat freshly baked.

Oat and Raspberry Ice-cream (serves 10) ♡

An exuberant dessert of a stunning pink. Serve on tea-plates or in glass sundae dishes with teaspoons. Make for a special occasion, and it will be memorable.

2oz (50g) porridge oats
2oz (50g) demerara sugar
3 egg whites
4oz (100g) caster sugar
½pt (300ml) double cream, lightly whipped to thicken
6oz (170g) raspberries, mashed with a fork

Method: Sprinkle the oats and demerara sugar into a Swiss roll tin or 2 sponge tins. Toast under a medium grill until golden, turning the tin(s) and stirring from time to time to allow even toasting. Put aside to cool. Put the egg whites into a large bowl. Whisk until stiff and able to stand in peaks. Whisk in the caster sugar by the heaped tablespoon until it has all been absorbed and the mixture is thick and glossy. Use a metal spoon to fold (not mix) in the cream and the cold oat mixture. Lastly, fold in the raspberries. Turn into a 2pt (1.2 litre) freezer-proof basin. Cover and freeze for several hours until solid.

Oat and Cashew Ice-cream (serves 10 as a dessert, or as a topping for 30 desserts) ♡

An interesting texture and an even more interesting taste. Makes an extra-special dessert for a special occasion. Serve in glass dishes with a teaspoon.

2oz (50g) cashew nuts
3oz (75g) porridge oats
2oz (50g) demerara sugar
3 egg whites
4oz (100g) caster sugar
½pt (300ml) double cream, lightly whipped to thicken

Method: Finely chop the nuts. Sprinkle into a Swiss roll tin or 2 sponge tins. Cover with the oats and sprinkle with the demerara sugar. Toast under a medium grill, turning the tin(s) and stirring from time to time to allow even toasting. When golden, put aside to cool. Put the egg whites into a large bowl. Whisk until stiff and able to stand in peaks. Whisk in the caster sugar by the heaped tablespoon until it has all been absorbed and the mixture is thick and glossy. Use a metal spoon to fold (not mix) in the cream and the cold oat mixture. Turn into a 2-pt (1.2 litre) freezer-proof basin. Cover and freeze for several hours, until solid. Serve as a dessert, with wafer biscuits and fresh fruit to decorate; or put scoopfuls on top of fruit salad or fruit instead of cream.

NOTE: The flavour of this ice-cream will combine well with any kind of ripe fresh fruit: slices of peeled peach, plums, pawpaw or pineapple, raspberries, strawberries or blueberries. But choose fruit with a bright colour, as the ice-cream is oatmeal-coloured and can look dreary with fruit such as banana, apple or pear.

Atholl Brose (3 or 4 servings) ♡

A traditional sweet from Scotland, for grown-ups. It is rather rich, so serve it in modest portions.

- 1 heaped tablespoon medium oatmeal
- 1 tablespoon chopped almonds
- 5fl oz (150ml) whipping cream
- 2 tablespoons whisky
- 2 teaspoons lemon juice
- 1 generous tablespoon runny honey
- 2 lemon slices for finishing

Method: Sprinkle the oatmeal into a sponge tin with the almonds. Put under a medium grill until it turns light brown, turning the tin round so it is evenly toasted. Put aside to cool on a plate. Whip the cream until it has thickened and will stand in peaks. Using a fork, lightly whisk in the whisky, lemon juice and honey. Fold in (don't mix or beat) the toasted oatmeal mixture. Pile into 4 wine or sundae glasses and put in the fridge to chill. Decorate with half-slices of lemon, and serve on saucers with teaspoons.

Cream Crowdie (serves 3 or 4) ♡

A dazzling dessert with a variety of textures—the oatmeal is delightfully crunchy in contrast with the soft fruit and cream.

- 1oz (25g) pinhead (coarse) oatmeal
- 5fl oz (150ml) whipping cream
- 1oz (25g) caster sugar
- 2 teaspoons rum
- 4oz (100g) fresh raspberries

Method: Sprinkle the oatmeal into a sponge tin. Put under a medium grill until it turns light brown, turning the tin round so it is evenly toasted. Put aside on a plate to cool. Pour the cream into a basin and whip until it will stand up in soft peaks. Whisk in the sugar and rum with a fork. Fold in the prepared oatmeal and the raspberries carefully, so as not to damage the fruit. Pile into individual serving glasses and chill in the fridge for at least 2 hours before serving.

NOTE: Watch over the toasting oatmeal carefully. It must not be allowed to brown too much or burn.

Fruit Crunch Dessert (serves 2) ♡♡

A crisp, golden topping to sprinkle over stewed or baked fruit. It can be dressed up in glass dishes for a dinner party or served in a bowl as an everyday pudding. The crunchiness of the topping contrasts with the soft texture of the fruit.

1oz (25g) polyunsaturated margarine
2½oz (65g) porridge oats
2 level tablespoons demerara sugar
1 level tablespoon desiccated coconut
1 level tablespoon slivered almonds
1 teaspoon sesame seeds

Method: Put the margarine into a heavy-based frying pan and melt gently until runny. Sprinkle in the oats, sugar, coconut, almonds and sesame seeds. Stir while you cook for 3 or 4 minutes until the mixture becomes golden and crisp. Have ready hot stewed or baked fruit (see below), sweetened to taste. Spoon it into 2 dishes or bowls. Sprinkle with the topping mixture and serve with a tablespoon of natural yoghurt or, for a special occasion, a tablespoon of cream.

NOTE: The fruit base should be just nicely moist to take the crunchy topping. You may need to drain it if there is too much juice. Sliver the almonds by cutting them lengthways into thin slices with a large, sharp knife.

Fruit base suggestions

apple and summerfruits
cooking-apple
apricot and apple
apricots
blackberry and apple
peach and raspberry
peaches
pears
plum and apple
plums

Spicy Oat Crumble (4 servings) ♡♡♡

The spice gives a great lift to ordinary crumble. Try this plum version:

Base

1lb (500g) firm ripe plums (e.g. Victorias) or other fruit (see below)
2 tablespoons water
1 tablespoon demerara sugar

Topping

4oz (100g) plain wholewheat flour
½ level teaspoon cinnamon
3oz (75g) polyunsaturated margarine
1 heaped tablespoon demerara sugar
2oz (50g) porridge oats

Preheat oven: Gas 5/375°F/190°C/fan oven 170°C
Position: above centre shelf
Baking time: about 30 minutes/fan oven 20 minutes

Method: Cut the plums in half and remove the stones. Grease a pie dish and cover the base with the prepared plums. Sprinkle the water over and then the sugar. Put the flour into a bowl with the spice. Mix well. Add the margarine and rub in with the fingertips until the mixture resembles breadcrumbs. Stir in the sugar and oats. Spoon over the plums and press flat. Make a hole in the centre through to the fruit, then bake until golden brown. Serve hot with yoghurt, single cream or custard.

Variations

- apple and summerfruits
- cooking-apples
- apricots
- apricots, apple and raspberries
- blackberry and apple
- gooseberries
- greengages
- peaches
- cooking-pears

Baked Apples with Oat Stuffing (4 servings) ♡♡♡♡

Baked stuffed apples are less likely to collapse during cooking than ones with cavities. Serve this traditional pudding during winter. Bramley seedlings are the best apples for this recipe.

4 medium-sized cooking apples
water
demerara sugar for sprinkling

Filling

1 heaped tablespoon porridge oats
2 teaspoons demerara sugar
½ tablespoon soft butter
1 heaped tablespoon sultanas
3 pinches cinnamon
rind of ¼ lemon, finely grated

Preheat oven: Gas 4/350°F/180°C/fan oven 160°C
Position: about centre shelf
Baking time: about 30 minutes/fan oven about 20 minutes

Method: Wash the apples. Remove cores with an apple corer so that you have a central hole right through. With a sharp knife score a line around the middle of each apple, to allow the flesh to expand during baking without bursting the skin. In a basin, mix all the ingredients for the filling. Divide the mixture into four and fill the central cavity of each apple. Put the apples into an ovenproof dish. Pour in enough water to come ¼ of the way up the apples. Sprinkle with the demerara sugar. Bake until the top halves of the apples are brown and crisp and the flesh light and fluffy. Serve in individual bowls with a little of the cooking juice.

SWEET OAT PANCAKES ♡♡♡

For the basic oat pancake recipe, see p. 42. Pancakes make a good pudding and can be varied with different fillings.

Jam Pancake

Warm a little jam in a small saucepan. Add a squeeze of lemon juice, then spread the mixture over the pancakes. Roll up and serve on warm plates with a light dusting of caster sugar. Any homemade jam is ideal, but commercially made apricot, strawberry, blackcurrant or raspberry jam, or fresh chopped blueberries, won't disappoint for this simple pudding.

Mashed-fruit Pancake

Soft fruits lend themselves to mashing and spreading. Try ripe strawberries, raspberries, loganberries, kiwi-fruit and banana. If they are not sweet enough, sweeten to taste with a little caster sugar. Spread over the pancakes and roll up. Dust with caster sugar.

Fruit Pancakes

See pp. 42–3 for a wider selection of fillings.

Fruit Cobbler (3 servings) ♡♡♡

A hearty pudding for cold days. The scones on the top contrast nicely with the fruit base.

Base

- 12oz (350g) prepared fruit (see list below)
- water
- 2oz (50g) soft brown sugar

Cobbler

- 2oz (50g) self-raising flour
- 1oz (25g) rolled oats
- ½ level teaspoon baking powder
- ½ level teaspoon cinnamon or allspice
- 1oz (25g) polyunsaturated margarine
- ½oz (15g) soft brown sugar
- milk to bind and finish
- demerara sugar for finishing

Preheated oven: Gas 4/350°F/180°C/fan oven 160°C
Position: top shelf
Baking time: 30–35 minutes/fan oven 20–23 minutes

Method: Make the base. Put the fruit into an ovenproof dish. Sprinkle with about 2 tablespoons water and the sugar. Now make the topping. Put the flour, oats, baking powder and spice into a bowl. Mix well. Add the margarine and rub in with the fingertips. Sprinkle in the sugar and mix to a soft dough with a little milk. Put on to a floured worktop and roll out thickly (½in/1cm). Use a 2in (5cm) round cutter to make 6 or 7 rounds. Arrange them over the fruit, around the edge, slightly overlapping. Brush the scones with milk and sprinkle with demerara sugar. Bake until the scone topping is golden brown and the fruit soft. Serve warm with unflavoured yoghurt.

Fruit
Choose one of the following:
cooking-apples
blackberry and apple
plum
plum and apple
plum, apple and blackberry (autumn fruits)

Variations
Omit spice. For the base use one of the following:
- apple and fresh apricot
- apple and summerfruits
- fresh peach and raspberry

Rhubarb Oat Crumble (2 or 3 servings) ♡♡♡
A classic pudding for winter.

Base

12oz (350g) prepared rhubarb
1 tablespoon fresh lemon or orange juice
1 heaped tablespoon demerara sugar
rind of ½ lemon or orange, finely grated

Topping

1½oz (40g) plain flour
1 slightly heaped tablespoon rolled oats
1½oz (40g) polyunsaturated margarine
1oz (25g) demerara sugar

Preheat oven: Gas 4/350°F/180°C/fan oven 160°C
Position: top shelf
Baking time: 45 minutes/fan oven 30 minutes

Method: Cut the rhubarb into short pieces. Put into a greased ovenproof dish. Sprinkle with the fruit juice, sugar and rind. Now make the topping. Put the flour and oats into a bowl. Mix well and add the margarine. Rub in with the fingertips until the mixture resembles large crumbs. Stir in the sugar. Cover the fruit with the crumble mixture and make a hole in the centre through to the fruit. Bake until golden brown. Serve hot with natural yoghurt or just on its own.

Apple Oat Crumble ♡♡♡

Make as for rhubarb crumble but using sliced, peeled and cored cooking-apples instead of the rhubarb and lemon juice and rind.

Cheesecake (6 to 8 servings) ♡♡♡

Most cheesecakes are heavy on cream and whole eggs. This one is made without either, so it is considerably lower in fat. Makes a stunning dessert or a treat for a celebration tea.

6 digestive biscuits made with oatmeal (see recipe, p. 80)
1oz (25g) polyunsaturated margarine
rind of 1 orange, finely grated
juice of 1 orange
1 tablespoon fresh lemon juice
½oz (15g) sachet gelatine crystals
12oz (350g) cottage cheese
1 small carton unflavoured yoghurt
1½oz (40g) caster sugar
2 egg whites
fresh fruit for decoration

Method: Grease an 8in (20cm) flan ring and put it on a flat serving plate. Grind the biscuits to crumbs in a coffee grinder.

Melt the margarine gently in a small saucepan. Stir in the crumbs. When all the fat has been absorbed, sprinkle them inside the flan ring and press them down to form the base.

Put the orange rind into the blender. Pour the orange juice into a saucepan with the lemon juice. Heat, take off the hob and sprinkle in the gelatine. Stir until all the crystals have dissolved. Pour into the blender. Add the cheese, yoghurt and sugar. Blend until smooth, then spoon into a basin. Whisk the egg whites until stiff, then fold in the cheese mixture with a metal spoon until smooth again. Carefully spoon the mixture over the crumb base, levelling the top with a knife. Put into the fridge to set firm for an hour or more. When the cheesecake is ready to serve, take off the flan ring and decorate the top with fresh fruit—halved strawberries, whole raspberries, clusters of redcurrants, slices of peeled peach or kiwi-fruit.

CHAPTER 6

Sweet Biscuits and Cookies

Orange Oatmeal Biscuits (makes about 40) ♡♡

Crisp, dainty biscuits to serve with morning coffee, or with ice-cream and sorbet for dessert.

- 2oz (50g) fine oatmeal
- 2oz (50g) plain unbleached white flour
- ¼ level teaspoon bicarbonate of soda
- pinch salt
- 2oz (50g) polyunsaturated margarine
- 2oz (50g) caster sugar
- rind of ½ orange, finely grated
- juice of ½ orange

Preheat oven: Gas 5/375°F/190°C/fan oven 170°C
Position: top shelf
Baking time: 10 minutes/fan oven 7 minutes

Method: Mix the oatmeal, flour, bicarbonate of soda and salt in a bowl. In a second bowl cream the margarine and sugar. Beat until light and fluffy. Stir in the oatmeal mixture and the orange rind. Add enough orange juice to make a stiff paste.

Knead for a minute until smooth. Cut in half. Flour the worktop and roll out each half thinly. Cut into rounds with a large fluted cutter. Then cut each one in half with a sharp knife. Lift them with a spatula on to a baking sheet. Bake until pale gold, turning golden brown round the edges. Put on to a wire rack to cool and crisp. When cold, store in an airtight container. Best eaten freshly made.

Oat Munchies (makes 15 shortcake biscuits) ♡♡

These always turn out looking really professional; they are all the same size and shape (rectangular) although no cutter is used.

4oz (100g) self-raising flour	1 good pinch mixed spice
1oz (25g) porridge oats	2oz (50g) polyunsaturated margarine
1oz (25g) granulated sugar	½ tablespoon runny honey
1oz (25g) soft brown sugar	1 tablespoon milk
2 good pinches salt	

Preheat oven: Gas 6/400°F/200°C/fan oven 180°C
Position: top shelf
Baking time: 12–15 minutes/fan oven 8–10 minutes

Method: Put the flour, oats, sugars, salt and spice into a bowl. Mix well. Add the margarine and rub in with the fingertips until the mixture resembles coarse crumbs. Put the honey into a cup with the milk and stir with a teaspoon until they have combined. Add to the flour mixture and mix to a stiff dough by hand. (Don't be tempted to add more liquid—keep mixing until 1 ball of dough is formed.) Knead lightly on a floured worktop and form into a large sausage (about 2in (5cm) in diameter). Flatten slightly along its length and use a large sharp knife to cut off ¼in (5mm) thick slices.

Have ready a greased baking sheet. Place the biscuits on it, spaced well apart. Bake until golden brown and textured on top. Take out of the oven. Leave on the baking sheet for a minute, then remove with a spatula and place on a wire rack to cool. When cold they will be crisp. Store in an airtight container, and eat within a week.

Oat Crisps (makes 12) ♡♡

Thin, delicate, golden biscuits for elevenses or tea.

- 2oz (50g) polyunsaturated margarine
- 2oz (50g) caster sugar
- 2oz (50g) porridge oats
- ½ teaspoon almond flavouring

Preheat oven: Gas 6/400°F/200°C/fan oven 180°C
Position: top shelf
Baking time: about 10 minutes/fan oven about 7 minutes

Method: Put the margarine and sugar into a bowl. Mix/beat to a cream. Add the oats and flavouring. Mix well by hand until one ball of dough has formed. Break off pieces the size of a walnut, and roll between the palms to form balls. Have ready a greased baking sheet. Place the balls on it, leaving plenty of space around each one for them to spread. Flatten slightly and bake until golden brown. Leave on the baking sheet for 5 minutes, then loosen carefully with a spatula and transfer to a wire rack to cool and crisp. Eat freshly baked.

NOTE: During baking the biscuits will spread to 3in (7.5cm) in diameter.

Oat and Sesame Biscuits (makes 12) ♡♡♡

Surprisingly dainty round biscuits, pale golden and with an attractive texture.

- 1 tablespoon toasted sesame seeds
- 1½oz (40g) porridge oats
- 1oz (25g) medium oatmeal
- 1½oz (40g) soft brown sugar
- 3 tablespoons sunflower oil
- ½ beaten egg

Preheat oven: Gas 3/325°F/160°C/fan oven 140°C
Position: top shelf
Baking time: about 15 minutes/fan oven 10 minutes

Method: Put all ingredients except the egg into a bowl. Mix thoroughly and leave to stand for about an hour. Add the egg and mix well. Have ready a greased baking sheet. Use 2 teaspoons to place 12 heaped teaspoonfuls of the mixture on to it, spaced well apart. Flatten with the back of the teaspoon. Bake until golden. Leave on the baking sheet for 2 or 3 minutes, then lift off with a spatula and cool on a wire rack. Store in an airtight container and eat within a week.

NOTE: To toast sesame seeds, sprinkle them into a heavy-based frying pan. Put over a medium heat, stirring every few seconds until they begin to pop and turn brown. Leave to cool before using.

Digestive Biscuits (makes about 12) ♡♡♡♡

A classic biscuit, semi-sweet, high in fibre but low in fat and sugar. (Do not confuse with commercial versions, which are usually high in sugar, fat and salt.) Ideal on their own as a snack or with cheese, they are an aid to digestion—hence the name.

2oz (50g) medium oatmeal
4oz (100g) plain wholewheat flour
tiny pinch powdered cloves
2oz (50g) polyunsaturated margarine
1½oz (40g) soft brown sugar
½ beaten egg
milk to mix

Preheat oven: Gas 6/400°F/200°C/fan oven 180°C
Position: centre shelf
Baking time: 15–18 minutes/fan oven 10–12 minutes

Method: Put the oatmeal, flour and cloves into a bowl. Mix well. Add the margarine and rub in with the fingers until the mixture resembles breadcrumbs. Sprinkle in the sugar and stir with a knife. Make a well in the centre. Pour in the egg and a little milk. Use a wooden spoon to mix to a stiff paste, adding more milk if required. Knead lightly on a floured worktop for a minute. Roll out to about in (3mm) thick. Prick all over with a fork and cut into rounds with a biscuit cutter or tumbler. Use a spatula to place them on greased baking sheets. Bake.

Put on to a wire rack to cool and crisp. When cold, store in an airtight container.

Chocolate Digestives ♡♡

Make as for digestive biscuits. Spread on one side with melted cooking-chocolate and leave to set. For a texture, trail a fork across the chocolate before it sets.

Oat Cookies (makes 9) ♡♡

These quickly made cookies are halfway between a flapjack and a biscuit, yet still manage to look dainty. They keep well but are nicest freshly baked.

1oz (25g) polyunsaturated margarine
1 generous teaspoon golden syrup
1oz (25g) demerara sugar
1oz (25g) white self-raising flour
2 good pinches bicarbonate of soda
small pinch salt
1oz (25g) porridge oats
½ teaspoon ground almonds

Preheat oven: Gas 4/350°F/180°C/fan oven 160°C
Position: top shelf
Baking time: about 15 minutes/fan oven 10 minutes

Method: Put the margarine, sugar and syrup into a small pan. Heat gently while you stir, until the margarine has melted and the sugar dissolved. Take off the heat and leave to cool. Mix the flour, bicarbonate of soda, salt, oats and nuts in a bowl. Add the liquid from the pan and mix to a soft dough. When cool enough, break off pieces the size of a walnut and roll into balls. Space well apart on a greased baking sheet. Bake until spread and golden brown. Cool on the baking sheet for a minute, then loosen with a spatula and place carefully on a wire rack to cool and crisp. When completely cold, store in an airtight container. Eat within a week.

Melting Moments (makes about 9) ♡♡

Melt-in-the-mouth cookies with a coating of oats.

2½oz (65g) polyunsaturated margarine
1½oz (40g) caster sugar
1 tablespoon beaten egg
¼ teaspoon vanilla flavouring
½oz (15g) porridge oats
2oz (50g) self-raising flour
more porridge oats for finishing

Preheat oven: Gas 4/350°F/180°C/fan oven 160°C
Position: top shelf
Baking time: 20 minutes/fan oven 13 minutes

Method: Beat the margarine and sugar to a cream in a mixing bowl. When the mixture is light and fluffy, beat in the egg and flavouring. Sprinkle in the oats and flour. Stir with a wooden spoon to make a stiff dough. (If you have put in too much egg, sprinkle in more flour.) Break off walnut-sized pieces and roll into balls between the palms. Put about a heaped teaspoon of oats into a saucer. Roll each ball in the oats to coat, and place them on a greased baking sheet, well apart. Flatten each one a little and bake until golden. Leave on the baking sheet for 2 minutes, then put on a wire rack to grow cold. Store in an airtight container and eat within a week.

Oat and Nut Cookies (makes 16) ♡♡
Brown, knobbly, munchy cookies for a snack, elevenses or tea, or for the lunchbox. Wholesome and satisfying, but definitely not for slimmers.

2oz (50g) polyunsaturated margarine
1 tablespoon thick honey
3oz (75g) plain wholewheat flour
¾ level teaspoon baking powder
2oz (50g) ground nuts (see note)
few drops almond flavouring
1oz (25g) soft brown sugar
2oz (50g) porridge oats
pinch salt
1 egg, beaten

Preheat oven: Gas 4/350°F/180°C/fan oven 160°C
Position: top shelf
Baking time: about 20 minutes/fan oven 14 minutes

Method: Put the margarine into a medium saucepan with the

honey. Set over a gentle heat and stir until the margarine has melted. Mix the flour, baking powder, nuts, flavouring, sugar, oats and salt in a bowl, pour in the margarine and honey mixture, and stir well. Add the egg and mix to a thick, sticky consistency. With 2 teaspoons break off walnut-sized pieces and place on a greased baking sheet, spaced well apart. Flatten the little mounds slightly, and bake until brown. Put on a wire rack to cool. When cold, store in an airtight container. Eat within a week.

NOTE: Make up the 2oz (50g) mixture of nuts of your choice and grind in a coffee grinder. Use walnuts, almonds, cashews or a mixture, but avoid peanuts.

Oat and Carrot Cookies (makes 20) ♡♡♡

These modest little cookies are a delightful apricot colour with a refreshing flavour. Dainty enough for the tea table but filling enough for the lunchbox.

- 3oz (75g) soft brown sugar
- 3oz (75g) polyunsaturated margarine
- 2oz (50g) carrot, finely grated
- ½ beaten egg
- 1 teaspoon lemon rind, finely grated
- 2½oz (65g) plain flour
- good pinch salt
- 1 level teaspoon baking powder
- 2½oz (65g) porridge oats

Preheat oven: Gas 6/400°F/200°C/fan oven 180°C
Position: top shelf
Baking time: 15 minutes/fan oven 10 minutes

Method: Mix the sugar and margarine in a bowl. Beat to a soft cream. Add the carrot and egg. Mix, then beat well. Put in the rind, flour, salt and baking powder. Mix well. Finally, stir in the oats. Have ready a greased baking sheet. Use 2 teaspoons to put heaped teaspoons of the mixture on to it, leaving space around each one. Spread them out with the back of a teaspoon. Bake until they start to brown around the edges. Leave on the baking sheet for 2 minutes, then loosen with a spatula and transfer to a wire rack to cool. When completely cold, store in an airtight container. Eat within 5 days.

Oat Crunchies (makes 8) ♡♡

A no-nonsense kind of biscuit, easy and quick to make.

1½oz (40g) plain flour
¼ teaspoon bicarbonate of soda
1oz (25g) soft brown sugar
1½oz (40g) porridge oats
2 teaspoons milk
1½oz (40g) polyunsaturated margarine
1 really generous teaspoon golden syrup

Preheat oven: Gas 2/300°F/150°C/fan oven 130°C
Position: top shelf
Baking time: 30 minutes/fan oven 20 minutes

Method: Mix the flour and bicarbonate of soda in a bowl. Stir in the sugar and oats. Put the milk, margarine and syrup into a small saucepan. Gently heat while you stir until the margarine has melted. Cool for 5 minutes, off the heat, and stir in the dry oat mixture. Mix well with a wooden spoon, then knead by hand to form 1 lump of dough. Break off pieces the size of a walnut. Roll into balls between your palms. Place on a baking sheet, flatten and press into circles about 3in (7.5cm) across. Bake until they turn golden brown around the edges. Leave on the baking sheet for 3 minutes, then use a spatula to loosen and place them on a wire rack to cool. They will crisp as they cool down.

Vanilla Oat Wafers (makes about 16) ♡♡

2oz (50g) fine oatmeal
2oz (50g) plain unbleached white flour
pinch salt
¼ level teaspoon bicarbonate of soda
2oz (50g) polyunsaturated margarine
2oz (50g) caster sugar
¼ teaspoon vanilla flavouring, or more to taste
water
more plain flour for kneading

Preheat oven: Gas 5/375°F/190°C/fan oven 170°C

Position: top shelf
Baking time: 10 minutes/fan oven 7 minutes

Method: Put the oatmeal, flour, salt and bicarbonate of soda into a bowl. Mix well. In a second bowl mix/cream the margarine and sugar. Stir in the oatmeal mixture, flavouring and enough water to make a stiff paste. Using more flour, knead for a minute until smooth. Cut the dough into 4. Roll out each piece thinly on a floured worktop. Cut round a tea-plate to make 4 large rounds, then cut each round into four. Loosen carefully with a spatula and place on a greased baking sheet. Prick each one with a fork to make a pattern, and bake. When they turn brown round the edges, put them on a wire rack to cool. Serve freshly baked, if possible. After storage in an airtight container for a few days, they may need a re-crisp in the oven. Serve with ice cream or sorbets.

CHAPTER 7

Bread, Scones, Plain Biscuits and Crispbreads

NOTE: See p. 131 for notes on yeast.

Miniature Three-cereal Loaves (makes about 12) ♡♡♡

The large version of these tasty loaves is popular in Germany. They are characterised by their interesting taste—no sugar or fat added—their oval shape and the split top sprinkled with seeds. One of the three cereals is of course oatmeal, and you can use either medium or fine. Made in less than an hour.

½oz (15g) oatmeal
½oz (15g) linseeds
3oz (75g) rye flour
8oz (225g) strong white flour
3 good pinches salt
¼oz (7g) instant 'fast action' yeast
1 tablespoon low-fat dried milk granules
7½oz (210ml) lukewarm water
more white flour for kneading
milk and sesame seeds for finishing

Preheat oven: Gas 7/425°F/220°C/fan oven 200°C

Position: top shelf
Baking time: about 15 minutes/fan oven 10 minutes

Method: Have ready a warmed bowl. Put in the oatmeal, linseeds, flours, salt, yeast and dried milk. Mix well and add the water. Use a wooden spoon to stir to a firm dough. Turn out on to a floured worktop and knead well for 3 or 4 minutes until smooth and elastic. Roll into a large, firm sausage and cut in half, then cut each half into 6 equal-sized pieces. Shape into ovals and place on a greased baking sheet, leaving space for them to spread. Use a really sharp knife to slash each one lengthways. Brush with milk and sprinkle with sesame seeds. Leave to rise in a warm place until doubled in size and puffy. Bake. Put on a wire rack to cool. Eat freshly baked, or the following day crisped in a hot oven for 3 or 4 minutes.

Quick Oat Rolls (makes 8) ♡♡♡♡

The traditional way to make oatmeal rolls takes several hours, so it is not surprising they have become a rarity. Here is a quicker and easier method which will make a batch in less than an hour. Not only are they healthy, they are also nutty-flavoured, crisp and golden brown. And they don't need any shaping by hand as they magically transform into perfect ovals on the baking sheet, all by themselves. Unlike ordinary wheatflour rolls which quickly go stale, these rolls keep well and can be used the following day. With their low fat and salt content, plenty of fibre and lots of personality, they are a great staple for a healthy diet.

4oz (100g) rolled oats
8fl oz (225ml) warm milk
3oz (75g) strong white flour
3oz (75g) strong wholewheat flour
¼oz (7g) instant 'fast action' yeast
½ teaspoon salt
½ teaspoon sugar
1 tablespoon sunflower oil
warm water
more white flour for kneading

Preheat oven: Gas 7/425°F/220°C/fan oven 200°C
Position: top shelf

Baking time: about 15–20 minutes/fan oven 10–12 minutes

Method: grind the oats to a flour in a coffee grinder. Put into a bowl with the milk. Stir well and leave to stand for 10 minutes. In a separate bowl, mix the white and brown flours, yeast, salt, sugar and oil. Add the soaked oats and stir with a wooden spoon, adding 3 tablespoons of warm water to make a soft dough. (Add more if necessary.) Turn out on to a well floured worktop and knead for 3 minutes until smooth and elastic. Shape into a large sausage about 8in (20cm) long. Cut in half with a floured knife. Cut each piece into 4 equal-sized pieces, dust the cut edges with flour and place apart on a greased baking sheet, cut side down. (Don't be tempted to shape them—they will shape themselves.) Leave in a warm place to rise until doubled in size. Bake, turning down the heat to Gas 5/375°F/190°C/fan oven 170°C, after 10 minutes. A little before serving, transfer to a wire rack to cool.

NOTE: If using them the following day, store overnight wrapped in food film in an airtight container. Either warm up in the oven or serve split and toasted.

Soft Oat Bread (makes 3 small loaves) ♡♡♡♡

A soft-textured bread with a thin crust. In spite of a heavy feel to the dough the finished loaves are well risen and light. They will keep for several days, wrapped in greaseproof paper.

scant 15oz (450ml) water
1 heaped tablespoon low-fat dried milk granules
1oz (25g) polyunsaturated margarine
6oz (170g) porridge oats
12oz (350g) strong wholewheat flour
2oz (50g) plain white flour
¼ teaspoon salt
½oz (15g) instant 'fast action' yeast
2 level teaspoons sugar
2 teaspoons sunflower oil

Preheat oven: Gas 6/400°F/200°C/fan oven 180°C
Position: above centre shelf
Baking time: about 30 minutes/fan oven 20 minutes

Method: Put the water and dried milk into a small saucepan.

Add the margarine and set over a gentle heat. Stir until the margarine has melted. Take off the hob and leave to cool. Grind the oats to flour in a coffee grinder. Grease a large mixing bowl with margarine. Put in the oat flour, wholewheat and white flours, salt, yeast and sugar. Mix well to combine. Drizzle in the oil. Pour in the lukewarm milk mixture, using a wooden spoon, mix to a soft dough. Add a little warm water if it feels too dry, or more flour if too wet. Turn out on to a floured worktop and knead well for 3 or 4 minutes until the dough feels smooth. Pick up the dough with both hands, lift until level with your head, then slap it down with a bang on the worktop. Turn it over and repeat twice more. (This will encourage the yeast to work.) Divide into 3 equal pieces.

Have ready 3 greased 1lb (500g) loaf tins. Press the dough into the tins with the knuckles so as to fill the corners. Cover with food film and leave to rise in a warm place until doubled in size. Remove food film and bake for ten minutes, then turn the heat down to Gas 5/375°F/190°C/fan oven 170°C for another 20 minutes/fan oven 15 minutes. Turn out on to a wire rack to cool. (The loaves should sound hollow underneath when knocked with the knuckles.)

NOTE: The milk mixture must not be hotter than lukewarm, or it will kill the yeast and the dough will fail to rise.

Oat Harvest Loaf (makes 1 medium-sized loaf) ♡♡♡♡♡

Four grains are used to make this hearty brown loaf that keeps and slices well and has a really nutty flavour. The oats contribute to all these good qualities and give the loaf a fine, even texture.

4oz (100g) porridge oats
2oz (50g) rye flour
2oz (50g) barley flour
8oz (225g) plain wholewheat flour
½ level teaspoon salt
1 level teaspoon sugar
1 heaped tablespoon low-fat dried milk granules
¼oz (7g) sachet instant 'fast action' yeast
1 tablespoon sunflower oil
about 15fl oz (450ml) warm water
more wholewheat flour for kneading

Preheat oven: Gas 6/400°F/200°C/fan oven 180°C
Position: above centre shelf
Baking time: 35–40 minutes/fan oven 23–27 minutes

Method: Grind the oats to flour in a coffee grinder. Put into a bowl with the rye, barley and wholewheat flours, the salt, sugar, dried milk and yeast. Mix well. Drizzle in the oil and stir. Pour in enough water to make a stiff, sticky dough. Turn out on to a well floured worktop and knead for 3 or 4 minutes until smooth. Pick the dough up with both hands, lift until level with your head, then slap it down with a bang on the worktop. Turn it over and repeat three more times. Shape into a large, flat sausage. If there are any cracks, pinch them together. Dust with flour.

Have ready a greased 2lb (1kg) loaf tin. Press the dough into it with your knuckles, filling the corners and flattening the top. Take a sharp knife and make a central slash, lengthways. Cover the tin loosely with food film and leave in a warm place to rise and double in size. When the dough has risen above the top of the tin and the cut opened up, remove the food film and bake until golden. Turn out of the tin immediately. If it is done it will sound hollow when the bottom of the loaf is knocked with the knuckles. If it doesn't, take it out of the tin, put it back in the oven, and bake for a little longer. Cool on a wire rack.

Brown Malted Oat Bread (makes 2 medium loaves)
♡♡♡♡♡

Wholesome brown family loaves with an even texture that will slice thinly and make good toast. The malt rounds off the nutty flavour of the oatmeal. Good all-round, healthy bread.

1½lb (700g) strong wholewheat bread flour
2oz (50g) fine oatmeal
1 teaspoon salt
1 heaped tablespoon low-fat dried milk granules
¼oz (7g) instant 'fast action' dried yeast
1 tablespoon sunflower oil
1 tablespoon malt extract
1pt (600ml) warm water
1 tablespoon porridge oats for finishing

Preheat oven: Gas 7/425°F/220°C/fan oven 200°C
Position: centre shelf
Baking time: about 45 minutes

Method: Put the flour, oatmeal, salt, dried milk, yeast and oil into a bowl. Mix well. Stir the malt extract into the water until dissolved. Pour it over the flour mixture. Use a wooden spoon to mix to a soft dough. Knead on a floured worktop for 3 or 4 minutes until it begins to look smooth. Pick up the dough and slap it down hard on the worktop. Turn it over and repeat 3 more times. Cut in half with a knife. Shape each piece of dough into a fat sausage and press into 2 greased 2lb (1kg) loaf tins. Brush the tops with warm water and sprinkle with the oats. Leave in a warm place to rise. When the dough has reached the top of the tins, bake. After 15 minutes turn down the oven to Gas 5/375°F/190°C/fan oven 170°C and continue baking for another 30 minutes or so. Turn out of the tins and tap the bottom of the loaves with the back of a teaspoon. If it sounds hollow the loaves are done. If the sound is dull and heavy, take them out of the tins, put back in the oven, and bake for a few minutes more. Cool on a wire rack. Cut when cold. Store in a bread bin or crock.

Oat Flatbreads (makes 2) ♡♡♡♡♡

These are made without yeast and are a cross between a chapati and a poppadom. Serve with curries, salads or casseroles instead of ordinary bread. Slimmers will appreciate them as they are made without any fat at all.

1oz (25g) porridge oats
1oz (25g) plain wholewheat flour
2 good pinches salt
3 tablespoons water

Method: Make the oats into flour using a coffee grinder. Put into a bowl with the wholewheat flour and the salt. Mix and add the water. Mix to a stiff paste and knead for 1 minute on a floured worktop. Divide into two. Using more flour, roll out into thin circles. Heat a heavy-based frying pan. (Do not grease it.) Cook the flatbreads for 2 minutes, then turn them over and cook on the other side.

Oat and Apple Scones (makes 6) ♡♡♡♡

If any of these robust scones are left over they can be toasted the following day for breakfast, elevenses, tea or a snack.

- 1oz (25g) porridge oats
- 4oz (100g) plain flour
- 2½ level teaspoons baking powder
- 1½oz (40g) polyunsaturated margarine
- ½ cooking-apple
- 1 slightly heaped tablespoon brown sugar
- 2½fl oz (75ml) skimmed milk, or more
- milk to glaze and porridge oats for sprinkling

Preheat oven: Gas 7/425°F/220°C/fan oven 200°C
Position: top shelf
Baking time: 15–20 minutes/fan oven 10–15 minutes

Method: Grind the oats to flour in a coffee grinder. Put into a bowl with the plain flour and baking powder and mix well. Add the margarine and rub in with the fingers until the mixture resembles breadcrumbs. Peel and finely grate the apple. Add with the sugar to the flour mixture. Stir, pouring in enough milk to make a soft dough. Knead lightly. Sprinkle flour over a greased baking sheet. Place the lump of dough in the centre and, with floured hands, pat and shape it into a round, ¾in (2cm) thick. (The less you handle the dough, the lighter the scones will be.) Cut it in half with a floured knife, then cut each piece into 3 triangles. Slide them gently apart to leave space between and brush the tops with milk and sprinkle with oats. Bake until well risen and the oats are browning on top. Serve freshly baked, split and spread with polyunsaturated margarine or butter.

Cheese and Oat Scones (makes 6) ♡♡♡

These golden-brown scones can be served for breakfast, brunch or a hearty tea. Good with tomato soup and salads; good for the lunchbox and picnics, too.

1oz (25g) porridge oats
1oz (25g) plain wholewheat flour
2oz (50g) plain unbleached white flour
2 level teaspoons baking powder
1oz (25g) polyunsaturated margarine
1 heaped tablespoon Parmesan cheese, finely grated
1 teaspoon made French mustard
5 tablespoons milk

Preheat oven: Gas 8/450°F/230°C/fan oven 210°C
Position: top shelf
Baking time: about 12–15 minutes/fan oven 8–10 minutes

Method: Make the oats into flour using a coffee grinder. Put into a mixing bowl with the plain flour and the baking powder. Mix well, then rub in the margarine until the mixture resembles fine breadcrumbs. Sprinkle in the cheese and mix by hand to distribute evenly. Put the mustard into a cup and add 1 tablespoon of milk. Mix to a smooth cream. Add the remaining 4 tablespoons of milk and stir well. Make a well in the centre of the flour mixture and pour in the liquid. Mix by hand to a soft dough. Knead only for a few seconds into 1 ball of smooth dough. Place on a greased and floured baking sheet. Lightly pat, press and shape with your fingers to make a round ½in (1cm) thick. Flour a sharp knife and cut the round in half. Cut each piece into 3 wedges and pull apart. Bake, turning the heat down to Gas 7/425°F/220°C/fan oven 200°C after 5 minutes. When well risen and golden brown, cool on a wire rack. Serve still slightly warm, then split and butter.

Fruit and Oat Scones (makes 6) ♡♡♡

The ultimate tea-time scone, but just as good for elevenses or a snack. The topping is unusual and attractive.

1oz (25g) porridge oats
3oz (75g) self-raising flour (wholewheat or unbleached white)
pinch salt
3 good pinches mixed spice
1oz (25g) polyunsaturated margarine
1 level tablespoon caster or soft brown sugar
1oz (25g) dried fruit (see below)
about 2½fl oz (75ml) milk
milk and porridge oats for topping

Preheat oven: Gas 7/425°F/220°C/fan oven 200°C
Position: top shelf
Baking time: about 15 minutes/fan oven 10 minutes

Method: Make the 1oz (25g) oats into flour, using a coffee grinder. In a bowl, mix the oat flour, the self-raising flour, salt and spice. Rub in the margarine until the mixture resembles breadcrumbs. Stir in the sugar and fruit of your choice, using a knife. Make a well in the centre and pour in enough milk to make a soft dough, by hand. Knead lightly for 30 seconds and dust with flour. Have ready a greased baking sheet. Put the dough in the centre and shape into a flat round ½in (1cm) thick by pressing and patting with the fingers. (The less the dough is handled, the lighter the scones will be.) Brush the top with milk and sprinkle with oats. Use a sharp knife to cut in half, then cut each half into three wedges. Pull apart gently and bake until golden brown. Cool on a wire rack. Serve freshly baked for each person to split and butter. If serving at the table, arrange in a bread basket with a doily.

Oat Dropscones (makes 8) ♡♡♡

Serve these flat scones warm for tea or breakfast on a warm plate, covered with a cloth serviette. They are really a kind of quick bread and have been enjoyed for centuries, although not made to this particular recipe which includes oats.

- 1oz (25g) porridge oats
- 2oz (50g) plain flour
- ½ level teaspoon baking powder
- 1 pinch salt
- ½ beaten egg
- 5½fl oz (165ml) milk
- sunflower oil for greasing

Method: Grind the oats to flour in a coffee grinder. Put into a basin with the plain flour, the baking powder and salt. Mix, then make a well in the centre. Pour in the egg and about half the milk. Mix them and beat until absorbed. Beat in the remaining milk to make a smooth batter. Put a griddle over a medium heat. To oil the griddle, have by you a saucer with a little oil and a screw of kitchen paper. Stir the batter and drop tablespoons of it on to the hot griddle, allowing 1 tablespoon per dropscone. They will spread out to about 2½in (6.5cm) in diameter.

When bubbles appear, after a minute or so, flip the drop-scones over with a spatula and cook on the other side for a minute. Have ready a warm plate on which to stack the drop-scones, and cover with a clean tea-towel. Oil the griddle again, ready for the next batch. Serve warm with butter or polyunsaturated margarine and jam or honey.

NOTE: If you don't have a griddle (bakestone), use a heavy-based frying pan or pancake pan instead.

Oatmeal Biscuits (makes 12) ♡♡♡♡

Easily made plain biscuits, low in fat, sugar and salt, high in oats—what could be healthier?

- 1½oz (40g) polyunsaturated margarine
- 2½oz (65g) medium oatmeal
- 1½oz (40g) plain wholewheat flour
- 2 teaspoons soft brown sugar
- ¼ level teaspoon baking powder
- beaten egg, to bind
- more flour for rolling out

Preheat oven: Gas 3/325°F/160°C/fan oven 140°C
Position: top shelf
Baking time: about 15 minutes/fan oven about 10 minutes

Method: Melt the margarine gently in a small pan. Put to one side to cool. Mix the oatmeal, flour, sugar and baking powder in a bowl. Make a well in the centre and pour in the cooled margarine. Stir with a knife, adding enough beaten egg to make a stiff, sticky paste. Knead lightly on a floured worktop. Roll out thinly using more flour, pressing with your fingers when it cracks, to mend it. Cut out shapes with floured cutters or a tumbler. Using a spatula, lift on to a greased and floured baking sheet. Bake. Cool on a wire rack. The biscuits will grow crisp as they cool down. Store in an airtight container.

Bannocks (makes 6) ♡♡♡♡

A traditional oatmeal recipe. Eat warm spread with butter for breakfast or tea.

- 3½oz (90g) medium oatmeal
- 1 slightly heaped tablespoon plain wholewheat flour
- ¼ level teaspoon baking powder
- 1oz (25g) polyunsaturated margarine
- boiling water from the kettle
- more oatmeal for rolling out

Method: Put a griddle or heavy-based frying pan on to heat. Mix the oatmeal, flour and baking powder in a bowl. Rub in the margarine with the fingers until the mixture resembles breadcrumbs. Make a well in the centre and spoon in 2 tablespoons boiling water. Mix to a soft dough using a wooden spoon, adding more water if required. Sprinkle the worktop with oatmeal and knead the dough for 2 minutes. Roll out to ¼in (5mm) thick and cut into rounds or squares with a sharp cutter or knife. Place on the (ungreased) hot griddle over a gentle heat and cook for 5 minutes on each side. Eat freshly cooked.

Oat Crackers (makes about 36) ♡♡♡

Crisp and flaky, these biscuits go well with cheese.

- ¾oz (20g) porridge oats
- 1½oz (40g) unbleached white flour
- 2 pinches salt
- 1½oz (40g) polyunsaturated margarine
- 2 tablespoons cold water
- more flour for rolling out

Preheat oven: Gas 6/400°F/200°C/fan oven 180°C
Position: top shelf
Baking time: about 15 minutes/fan oven 10 minutes

Method: Grind the oats to flour in a coffee grinder. Put into a bowl with the white flour and the salt. Mix well. Add half the margarine and rub in with the fingers until the mixture resembles breadcrumbs. Put on to a floured worktop and knead until smooth for a minute or two. Leave to rest while you gently melt the other half of the margarine in a small pan over

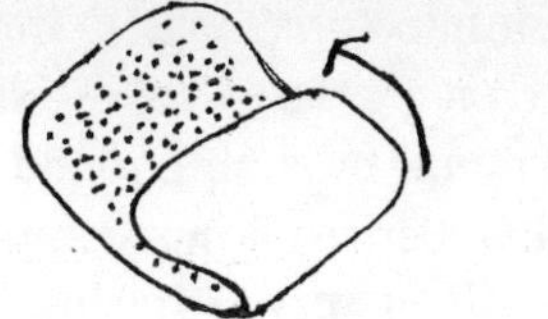
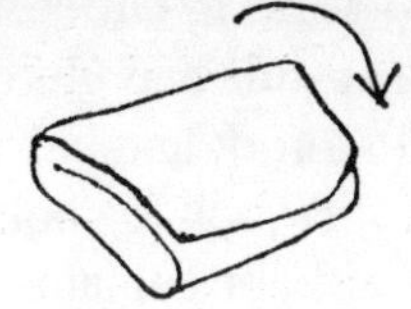

a low heat. Sprinkle the worktop with flour and roll out the dough thinly into a rectangle. Brush the top with melted margarine. Fold over one third and then the remaining third as shown. Roll out again thinly into a rectangle and repeat the process. Roll out once more as thinly as possible. Prick all over with a fork and cut into neat 2in (5cm) squares with a sharp knife or a pasta wheel. With a spatula, place the crackers on greased baking sheets and bake. When crisp and golden put them on a wire rack to cool. Store in an airtight tin.

Oat Crispbreads (makes 12) ♡♡♡♡

Thin, crisp and crunchy, to eat with cheese or use instead of bread. For a dinner party, make half-size crispbreads and bake for less time.

2oz (50g) fine oatmeal
2oz (50g) plain flour
¼ level teaspoon bicarbonate of soda
¼ level teaspoon salt
2oz (50g) polyunsaturated margarine
3 tablespoons water
more flour for kneading etc.

Preheat oven: Gas 5/375°F/190°C/fan oven 170°C
Position: top shelf
Baking time: 15 minutes/fan oven 10 minutes

Method: Put the oatmeal, flour, bicarbonate of soda and salt into a bowl. Mix well and add the margarine. Rub in with the fingertips until the mixture resembles breadcrumbs. Add the water and stir with a fork to make a sticky dough. Sprinkle with flour and knead for a minute to make a smooth dough. Divide in half. Roll out each half thinly on a floured worktop.

Use a sharp knife to cut each into 6 rectangles. Loosen carefully with a spatula and place on a greased baking sheet. Prick all over with a fork and bake until browning round the edges. Put on to a wire rack to cool and crisp. When completely cold store in an airtight container. Best served freshly baked, but can be re-crisped in the oven if necessary after storage. Eat within 10 days.

Sesame Oat Crispbreads ♡♡♡♡

Make as for oat crispbreads. Brush with milk and sprinkle with sesame seeds before baking.

Oatcakes (makes 12 crisp biscuits) ♡♡♡♡♡

Shop-bought oatcakes usually have a good deal of salt in them to prolong their shelf life. This can be avoided when baking at home.

4oz (100g) medium oatmeal
1oz (25g) plain flour
1 good pinch bicarbonate of soda
¼ teaspoon salt
1oz (25g) polyunsaturated margarine
about 1 tablespoon boiling water out of the kettle
more oatmeal for kneading

Preheat oven: Gas 5/375°F/190°C/fan oven 170°C
Position: top shelf
Baking time: about 20 minutes/fan oven about 14 minutes

Method: Put the oatmeal, flour, bicarbonate of soda and salt into a bowl. Mix well. Add the margarine and rub in with the fingertips until the mixture resembles breadcrumbs. Add the boiling water and mix with a knife to make a soft dough. Sprinkle the worktop with oatmeal and knead the dough until it can be rolled out. Divide into two. Using more oatmeal, roll out each piece into a circle ¼in (5mm) thick. Cut each circle in half with a sharp knife, then each half into 3 wedges. With a spatula, place the wedges on an ungreased baking sheet. Bake until crisp and dry. Transfer to a wire rack to grow cold.

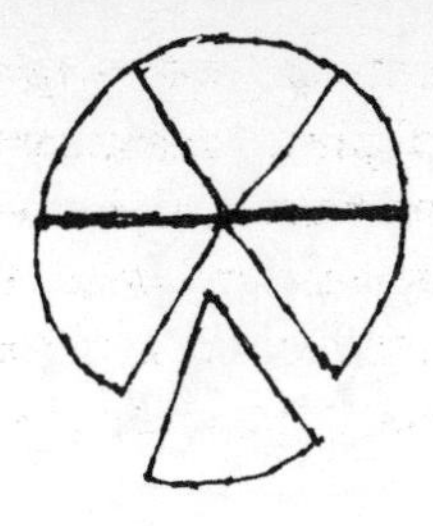

Serve with cheese or on their own. Store in an airtight container and use within a week.

Oat and Potato Crispbreads (makes about 20) ♡♡♡♡
These have all the characteristics of crispbreads minus the 'cardboardy' texture of shop-bought-ones designed to sit on the shelf for ages. Delightful with cheese or just on their own.

2oz (50g) plain flour
3 pinches salt
2oz (50g) porridge oats
1½oz (40g) polyunsaturated margarine
2oz (50g) mashed potato
more flour for rolling out

Preheat oven: Gas 3/325°F/160°C/fan oven 140°C
Position: top shelf
Baking time: 20–25 minutes/fan oven 13–17 minutes

Method: Mix the flour, salt and oats in a bowl. Add the margarine and rub in with the fingers until the mixture resembles coarse breadcrumbs. Put in the mashed potato and pull the mixture together to form 1 ball of dough. Knead for a minute until it feels smooth and quite firm. Lightly flour the worktop and roll the dough out thinly. Cut into squares or rectangles with a sharp knife. Using a spatula, place on baking sheets lightly dusted with flour. Bake until they begin to turn golden brown around the edges. Cool on a wire rack—as they cool down they will become crisp. Eat freshly baked or re-crisped in the oven after storing in an airtight container.

CHAPTER 8

Cakes, Buns and Teabreads

Ambrosia Cake ♡♡♡

The best time to eat this cake is when it is still warm. Enjoy for elevenses or tea-time, and as a pudding too. The texture of the golden top contrasts with the soft base.

Base

3oz (75g) porridge oats
3oz (75g) self-raising flour
2oz (50g) soft brown sugar
pinch salt
1 slightly heaped teaspoon baking powder
rind of ½ orange, finely grated
1 egg
5 tablespoons sunflower oil
4fl oz (125ml) skimmed milk

Topping

1½ (40g) soft brown sugar
1 tablespoon sunflower oil
1 large cooking-apple, finely grated
6 chopped dried apricot halves
1oz (25g) chopped almonds
1 tablespoon porridge oats

Preheat oven: Gas 4/350°F/180°C/fan oven 160°C

Position: top shelf
Baking time: 50 minutes/fan oven 35 minutes

Method: Grease a deep 7½in (19cm) square sponge tin. Line the base with greased greaseproof paper. Grind the 3oz (75g) oats to flour in a coffee grinder and put into a mixing bowl. Add the other flour, sugar, salt, baking powder and rind. Mix well. Break the egg into a basin and whisk. Stir in the oil and milk. Pour over the flour mixture and stir just enough to combine, being careful not to over-mix. Turn into the prepared tin and spread flat with a knife. Bake for 30 minutes.

Have ready the topping ingredients mixed in a basin. Take the cake out of the oven. Quickly spread the topping over it, as evenly as you can. Put back in the oven immediately. Lower the temperature to Gas 3/325°F/160°C/fan oven 140°C and bake for a further 20 minutes. Leave to cool in the tin for 15 minutes, then cut into 9 squares with a sharp knife. Serve still warm. Eat within 24 hours and store wrapped in food film to keep it moist.

Fruit-salad and Oat Cake ♡♡♡

This unusual cake is a real party piece. When cut the slices look particularly attractive because of the pale colours of the apricots, pears and apple set off by the black of the prunes. (The taste is quite different from the traditional type of fruitcake with currants, raisins and sultanas.)

8oz (225g) dried fruit salad (after stoning)
2oz (50g) porridge oats
6oz (170g) plain flour
4oz (100g) soft brown or caster sugar
1 tablespoon runny honey
4oz (100g) polyunsaturated soft margarine
2 level teaspoons baking powder
1 level teaspoon cinnamon
2 eggs
milk to mix
rind of 1 lemon, finely grated
flaked almonds for finishing

Preheat oven: Gas 4/350°F/180°C/fan oven 160°C
Position: centre shelf
Baking time: about 1¼ hours/fan oven 50 minutes

Method: Stone the prunes from the fruit salad. Chop all the fruit into raisin-sized pieces. Dust with flour to stop them sticking together. Grind the oats to flour in a coffee grinder. Put into a bowl with the plain flour, sugar, honey, margarine, baking powder, cinnamon and eggs. Mix/beat to a soft consistency, using a little milk if required. Stir in (don't beat) the prepared fruit and the rind. Have ready a greased 7in (18cm) cake tin, lined with greased greaseproof paper. Turn the mixture into the prepared tin and flatten the top with a knife. Scatter with the flaked almonds and bake. Test with a skewer to see if it is done. Leave in the tin for a few minutes before turning out on to a wire rack to cool. When completely cold, store in an airtight container. Use within 5 days.

NOTE: After stoning the prunes you may not have enough dried fruit salad to make 8oz (225g). Add chopped dried apricots or peaches.

Oat and Carrot Cake ♡♡♡♡

A moist cake that needs to be eaten within two days. High in fibre and, considering it is a cake, quite a healthy food.

- 2oz (50g) porridge oats
- ¼pt (150ml) water
- 3oz (75g) sultanas
- 3oz (75g) seedless raisins
- 4oz (100g) polyunsaturated margarine
- 6oz (170g) fresh carrot, finely grated
- 4oz (100g) soft brown sugar
- 5 tablespoons runny honey
- 4 pinches nutmeg
- 1 egg, beaten
- 6oz (170g) plain wholewheat flour
- 2 level teaspoons baking powder

Preheat oven: Gas 4/350°F/180°C/fan oven 160°C
Position: above centre shelf
Baking time: about 1 hour/fan oven about 40 minutes

Method: Grind the oats to flour in a coffee grinder. Put the water, dried fruit, margarine, carrot, sugar, honey and nutmeg into a large saucepan. While you stir, bring slowly to the boil. Lower the heat and simmer for 5 minutes, still stirring. Pour into a mixing bowl and leave to cool down (this could take up to 30 minutes). When the mixture is cold, stir in the egg. Sprinkle in the two flours and the baking powder. Stir in well. Have ready a greased and floured, round 9in (23cm) cake tin. Turn the mixture into it and bake. Test to see if it is ready by pressing with the fingers. If it springs back, it's done. Turn out of the tin and cool on a wire rack. Store in an airtight container and eat within 2 days of making.

Parkin (makes 10–12 pieces) ♡♡

A kind of oatmeal gingerbread popular in the north of England. The texture is coarse and, at first, fairly dry. It can be served in pieces as cake or sliced thickly and spread with butter or soft margarine like a bread. It needs to be kept in an airtight container for 2 or 3 days to develop, before cutting. By then it will be rich, moist, dark and shiny.

4oz (100g) polyunsaturated margarine
4oz (100g) soft brown sugar
4oz (100g) black treacle
4oz (100g) plain flour
pinch salt
½ level teaspoon bicarbonate of soda
1 level teaspoon mixed spice
1 level teaspoon ground ginger
4oz (100g) fine oatmeal
1 egg
5 tablespoons milk

Preheat oven: Gas 3/325°F/160°C/fan oven 140°C
Position: centre shelf
Baking time: about 1 hour/fan oven about 40 minutes

Method: Put the margarine, sugar and treacle into a large heavy-based saucepan. Heat gently while you stir, until the margarine has melted and the sugar dissolved. Take off the heat and leave to cool while you grease a 7in (18cm) square tin and line it with greased greaseproof paper. Put the flour into a bowl with the salt, bicarbonate of soda and spices. Mix well, then stir in the oatmeal. Make a well in the centre. Whisk the egg and milk in a basin. Add the cooled mixture from the saucepan. Whisk again and pour the mixture into the well.

Use a metal spoon to stir everything, until evenly mixed to a sloppy batter. Pour into the prepared tin and bake. When baked it will spring back if pressed lightly with the fingers. Leave in the tin to cool for 10 minutes, then remove the cake papers and turn out on to a wire rack. Cut with a sharp knife when cold. Store in an airtight container and eat within a week.

Variations

- *Orange Parkin* Omit spices. Instead, add the finely grated rind of 1 orange.
- *Lemon Parkin* Omit spices. Instead, add the finely grated rind of 1 lemon.
- *Honey Parkin* Instead of black treacle use runny honey.
- *Golden Parkin* Use golden syrup instead of black treacle.

Oat and Apple Cake (eggless) ♡♡♡

Serve for tea or elevenses, or as a pudding with custard or plain yoghurt.

2oz (50g) porridge oats
1 large cooking-apple
few drops lemon juice
4oz (100g) plain wholewheat flour
2 level teaspoons bicarbonate of soda
1 level teaspoon cream of tartar
pinch salt
4oz (100g) polyunsaturated margarine
4oz (100g) soft brown sugar
5fl oz (150ml) milk
rind of ½ lemon, finely grated

Preheat oven: Gas 4/350°F/180°C/fan oven 160°C
Position: above centre shelf
Baking time: about 45 minutes/fan oven about 30 minutes

Method: Make the oats into flour, using a coffee grinder. Peel and core the apple. Chop into small pieces and weigh out 4oz (100g). Sprinkle with the lemon juice, to stop discoloration. Grease a round 8in (20cm) sponge tin. Line the base with greased greaseproof paper. In a large bowl mix the flours, bicarbonate of soda, cream of tartar and salt. Rub in the margarine until the mixture resembles fine breadcrumbs. Stir in the sugar. Make a well in the centre and pour in the milk. Add the apple and the rind. Use a metal spoon to fold the ingredients together (do this as lightly as you can). Turn into the prepared tin and flatten with the back of the spoon. Bake. Leave in the tin for 4 or 5 minutes, then run a knife round the edge. Turn on to a wire rack to cool. Eat within 2 days. Store overnight, wrapped, in the fridge.

Oat, Date and Spice Cake (eggless) ♡♡♡

This is a useful recipe which makes a snack for elevenses, a quick cake for tea or a hearty pudding to serve with custard.

- 2oz (50g) porridge oats
- 2½oz (65g) plain wholewheat flour
- 1 heaped teaspoon baking powder
- 1 level teaspoon ground ginger
- 3 good pinches ground nutmeg
- 2½oz (65g) polyunsaturated margarine
- 3oz (75g) soft brown sugar
- 1 small cooking-apple, peeled and finely grated
- ¼pt (150ml) skimmed milk
- 2oz (50g) stoned, chopped dates, dusted with flour

Preheat oven: Gas 5/375°F/190°C/fan oven 170°C
Position: above centre shelf
Baking time: about 30 minutes/fan oven about 20 minutes

Method: Grease a square 7½in (19cm) sponge tin and line with greased greaseproof paper. Grind the oats to flour in a coffee grinder. Mix with the wholewheat flour, baking powder and spices in a large bowl. Add the margarine and rub in with the fingers until the mixture resembles breadcrumbs. Put in the sugar, grated apple and milk. Mix, then beat to a sloppy consistency. Stir in the dates. Turn into the prepared tin and spread flat with a knife. bake. (Test with a skewer to see if it is done.) Leave in the tin for a few minutes, then turn out carefully to cool on a wire rack. Peel off the paper and cut into 9 squares. Best eaten warm or on the day of baking.

Oat and Honey Fruit Cake ♡♡♡

An unusual fruit-cake with honey and nuts. The lattice pattern on the top tells you this cake contains oats—otherwise, you would never know. Practise making the lines of oats on a plate first.

2oz (50g) porridge oats
6oz (170g) plain wholewheat flour
3 level teaspoons baking powder
4oz (100g) polyunsaturated margarine
1 slightly rounded tablespoon soft brown sugar
4oz (100g) mixed dried fruit
3 rounded tablespoons runny honey
2 eggs, beaten
1oz (25g) chopped nuts
4 tablespoons milk
porridge oats for topping

Preheat oven: Gas 4/350°F/180°C/fan oven 160°C
Position: about centre shelf
Baking time: about 1 hour 10 minutes/fan oven about 50 minutes

Method: Make the oats into flour, using a coffee grinder. Put into a bowl with the wholewheat flour and the baking powder. Mix well and add the margarine, rubbing in with the fingertips until the mixture resembles breadcrumbs. Add the sugar, dried fruit, honey, eggs, nuts and milk. Mix well and turn into a greased 7in (18cm) square tin. Smooth flat with a knife and sprinkle with lines of oats to make the lattice. When ready, the cake will feel springy and firm to the touch. Leave in the tin for 5 minutes, then turn out on to a wire rack to cool. Best eaten freshly baked, still warm.

NOTE: This cake makes a good winter pudding served warm from the oven with hot custard.

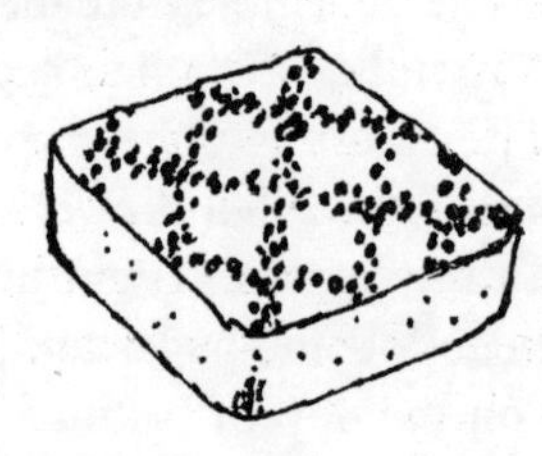

Millennium Buns (makes about 10) ♡♡♡

Light yeasted buns with oats and fresh fruit (see below for suggestions). An elevenses or snack food to eat freshly baked.

Dough

2oz (50g) polyunsaturated margarine
¼oz (7g) instant 'fast action' yeast
8oz (225g) strong white flour
1oz (25g) demerara sugar
rind of ½ lemon, finely grated
½ level teaspoon mixed spice
1 egg, lightly whisked
warm skimmed milk

Filling

1½oz (40g) polyunsaturated margarine
few drops almond flavouring
1 banana, sliced and chopped
1½oz (40g) demerara sugar
½oz (15g) ground almonds
1oz (25g) porridge oats

Topping

demerara sugar

Preheat oven: Gas 7/425°F/220°C/fan oven 200°C
Position: top shelf
Baking time: 12–15 minutes/fan oven 8–10 minutes

Method: First make the dough. Melt the margarine in a small saucepan and leave to cool. Mix the yeast, flour, sugar, lemon rind and spice in a bowl. Pour in the egg, cooled margarine and 4 tablespoons warm milk. Mix to a soft dough, adding a little more milk if required. Knead on a floured worktop for 3 or 4 minutes until smooth. Roll out, or press out with the fingers, into a rectangle about 10 × 14in (25 × 35cm). Now make the filling. Melt the margarine in a small saucepan, and stir in the almond flavouring. Brush the mixture liberally all over the dough. Mix the banana sugar, nuts and oats in a basin. Spread over the dough right to the edges, as evenly as you can. Starting with a short edge, roll up like a Swiss roll, then pinch the join together all the way along. With a sharp knife cut it into about 10 slices.

Have ready a greased baking sheet. Place the buns on it with space around each one. Cover loosely with food film and leave to rise in a warm place. When doubled in size and puffy, sprinkle a little demerara sugar over the top of each one. Bake until golden. Take out of the oven and loosen with a spatula. Cool a little on a wire rack and serve warm.

Variations
As fresh fruit is available all year round, other fruit can be used instead of banana. You will need 3oz (75g) prepared fruit. If the fruit is sour, increase the sugar in the topping. Choose one kind of fruit from the following:

- apricots, stoned and chopped
- blackberries, quartered
- blackcurrants, topped and tailed
- blueberries, halved
- gooseberries, topped and tailed, then quartered
- seedless grapes, quartered
- nectarines, stoned and chopped
- peaches, peeled, stoned and chopped
- pineapple, prepared and chopped
- plums, chopped and stoned
- small raspberries, halved

Oat Hot-cross Buns (makes 12) ♡♡♡
Although the oats cannot be detected in the buns themselves, the crosses open up to show the toasted oats used for finishing. Expect enthusiasm for this variation on the traditional Easter bun.

2oz (50g) polyunsaturated margarine
4oz (100g) porridge oats
8oz (225g) plain flour
½oz (15g) instant 'fast action' yeast
2oz (50g) caster sugar
4oz (100g) currants
½ level teaspoon cinnamon
½ level teaspoon mixed spice
3 good pinches grated nutmeg
rind of 1 lemon and 1 orange, finely grated
1 egg, beaten
¼pt (150ml) warm milk
oats for finishing
sugar glaze (see below)

Glaze
Use a small saucepan to boil 1 tablespoon each of milk, sugar and water.

Preheat oven: Gas 7/425°F/220°C/fan oven 200°C
Position: top shelf
Baking time: about 15–20 minutes/fan oven 10–15 minutes

Method: Melt the margarine gently in a small pan. Leave to cool. Grind the oats to flour in a coffee grinder. Put into a bowl with the yeast, the other flour, the sugar, currants, spices and rinds. Mix well. In a basin beat the cooled margarine, egg and milk with a fork. Pour this over the flour mixture. Use a wooden spoon to make a soft dough, adding a little more milk if required. Knead lightly on a floured worktop. Shape into a large sausage and cut into 6 equal-sized pieces. Roll/shape each one into a flattened ball and place on a greased baking sheet. Leave space for them to increase in size. Using a floured knife, cut each one with a cross. Sprinkle oats sparingly into the cuts and leave to double in size in a warm place. When they appear well risen and puffy, bake. Immediately they are out of the oven, put them on a wire rack to cool. Have ready the sugar glaze and brush the tops, avoiding the crosses. Eat freshly baked, split and spread with butter or margarine. Left-over buns can be toasted the following day.

West Country Oat Buns (makes 6 large flattish buns) ♡♡♡
With their textured tops, these are a variation of the classic Bath bun. The sweet, golden yeasted dough is enriched with eggs, sultanas and lemon rind. Serve for tea or elevenses, or as a snack, split and buttered. Eat these substantial but light buns freshly baked, or the following day, toasted.

2oz (50g) polyunsaturated margarine
4fl oz (125ml) cold milk
2oz (50g) porridge oats
¼ (7g) instant 'fast action' yeast
6oz (170g) plain flour
1oz (25g) caster sugar
3oz (75g) sultanas
rind of ½ lemon, finely grated
1 egg, beaten

Topping

1 tablespoon milk
¼ beaten egg
porridge oats
granulated sugar

Preheat oven: Gas 5/375°F/190°C/fan oven 170°C
Position: top shelf
Baking time: about 15 minutes/fan oven about 10 minutes

Method: Melt the margarine gently in a small pan. Take off the heat and pour in the cold milk. Mix well and leave to cool. Make the oats into flour, using a coffee grinder. Put into a bowl with the yeast, the other flour, the sugar, fruit and rind. Mix together and make a well in the centre. Pour in the margarine/milk and the beaten egg. Using a wooden spoon, mix to a stiff dough, adding a little more milk if required. Knead on a floured worktop for 2 minutes, until smooth. Shape into a large sausage. Cut in half, then cut each half into 3 equal-sized pieces. Shape into balls, flatten between your palms and place on a greased baking sheet, leaving plenty of space around each one.

Now make the topping. Whisk the egg and milk in a cup, using a fork. Brush this over the buns. Scatter sparingly with oats and sprinkle with sugar. Leave in a warm place to spread and double in size. When well risen and puffy, bake. Put immediately on to a wire rack to cool. Serve still warm.

Oat Rock Cakes (makes 12) ♡♡♡

Quick to make and bake, these little cakes are good for a snack or for tea and will travel well in a lunchbox. The oats help to keep them moist, but they are by nature dryish as they contain little fat and egg.

2oz (50g) porridge oats
4oz (100g) plain flour
1 level teaspoon baking powder
¼ teaspoon grated nutmeg
¼ teaspoon mixed spice
2½oz (65g) polyunsaturated margarine
3oz (75g) caster sugar
5oz (135g) mixed dried fruit
grated rind of 1 lemon
1 egg, beaten
milk to mix
granulated sugar and porridge oats for finishing

Preheat oven: Gas 5/375°F/190°C/fan oven 170°C
Position: above centre shelf
Baking time: 15 to 20 minutes/fan oven 10–12 minutes

Grind the oats to flour in a coffee grinder. Put into a bowl with the other flour, baking powder and spices. Mix and add the margarine. Rub in with the fingertips until the mixture resembles breadcrumbs. Sprinkle in the sugar, fruit and rind. Mix again. Using a knife, stir in the egg and enough milk to make a stiff mixture. Have ready a greased and floured baking sheet. Spoon the mixture on in heaps, leaving space around each one for them to spread during baking. Sprinkle the tops with sugar and a few oats to make a crispy top. Bake. Remove with a spatula and put on to a wire rack to cool. Serve still warm if possible. When completely cold, store in an airtight tin, individually wrapped in food film to keep them fresh. Use within 3 days.

NOTE: Avoid overbaking, or they will be too dry. To keep the cakes light, mix and stir, but don't beat as this toughens the texture.

Oat Sponge Buns (makes 6) ♡♡

These quickly made little buns, being more substantial than those made with all wheat flour, are more satisfying. Serve for tea, elevenses or as a snack. Wrap individually and add to lunchboxes. Ring the changes with 20 different flavours.

2oz (50g) polyunsaturated margarine
2oz (50g) caster sugar
½oz (15g) porridge oats
2oz (50g) self-raising flour
2 good pinches baking powder
1 egg
flavouring (see below)
milk to mix

Preheat oven: Gas 5/375°F/190°C/fan oven 170°C
Position: top shelf
Baking time: 12–15 minutes/fan oven 8–10 minutes

Method: Put all the ingredients into a bowl and mix/beat to a creamy consistency, adding a little milk if it is too stiff. Have ready a patty tin lined with 6 cake papers. Using 2 teaspoons together, fill the papers ¾ full, and bake. Take out of the tins and put on a wire rack to cool. Eat within 2 days of baking.

Flavours
Choose *one* of the following:

Almond—1 heaped teaspoon ground almonds and 3 or 4 drops almond flavouring
Dried apricot—4 dried apricot halves chopped into small pieces
Caraway—1 level teaspoon caraway seeds
Fresh cherries—6 sweet cherries, stoned and chopped
Chocolate—1 heaped teaspoon cocoa and 3 drops vanilla flavouring
Cinnamon—½ level teaspoon cinnamon
Coffee—1 level teaspoon instant coffee granules mixed with 2 teaspoons boiling water
Currants—1 heaped tablespoon currants and ½ level teaspoon lemon rind, finely grated
Mixed dried fruit—1 heaped tablespoon mixed dried fruit and 2 good pinches mixed spice
Ginger—½ teaspoon dried ginger
Lemon—finely grated rind of ½ lemon
Orange—finely grated rind of ½ orange
Dried peach—3 dried peach halves chopped into small pieces
Fresh peach—½ a ripe peach, peeled, then chopped into small pieces, and 3 drops vanilla flavouring
Fresh plum—2 ripe-eating plums, stoned, then chopped into small pieces, and 2 good pinches cinnamon
Seedless raisins—1 heaped tablespoon seedless raisins, chopped

Raspberry—6–8 fresh or frozen defrosted raspberries, chopped
Strawberry—about 4 medium-sized fresh strawberries chopped into small pieces
Sultanas—1 heaped tablespoon sultanas
Vanilla—few drops vanilla flavouring

Oat and Treacle Bread (makes 1 medium loaf) ♡♡♡
A light, even-textured brown teabread with an unusual flavour.

6oz (170g) plain wholewheat flour
6oz (170g) strong white flour
1½oz (40g) porridge oats
¼ teaspoon salt
1 heaped tablespoon low-fat dried milk granules
¼oz (7g) instant 'fast action' yeast
½oz (15g) polyunsaturated margarine
½pt (300ml) warm water
1 slightly rounded tablespoon golden syrup
porridge oats for topping

Preheat oven: Gas 6/400°F/200°C/fan oven 180°C
Position: above centre shelf
Baking time: about 35–40 minutes/fan oven about 23–26 minutes

Method: Put the flour, oats, salt and dried milk into a bowl. Mix well. Sprinkle in the yeast and mix again. Add the margarine and rub in with the fingertips. Pour about half the water into a basin. Stir in the syrup until completely dissolved in the water. Pour into the flour mixture and mix by hand, adding the remaining water to make a soft dough. Knead on a floured worktop for 3 or 4 minutes, then shape into a fat sausage. Have ready-greased a 2lb (1kg) loaf tin. Press the dough into it with the knuckles, to fill the corners. Brush the top with warm water and sprinkle with a few oats to give a speckled finish. Put in a warm place to rise. When the dough has reached the top of the tin, bake. Turn out on to a wire rack to cool. Serve sliced and buttered. Store as for bread.

Dark Oat and Treacle Bread ♡♡♡

Make as for oat and treacle bread but use black treacle instead of golden syrup.

Muesli Bread (makes 1 small loaf) ♡♡♡♡

This is the ultimate round-the-clock teabread. Brown, nutty, fruity and nourishing.

- ¼oz (7g) instant 'fast action' yeast
- 1 heaped tablespoon soft brown sugar
- 5oz (135g) plain wholewheat flour
- 1oz (25g) strong white flour
- 1 heaped tablespoon sultanas
- 2 dried apricot halves, chopped into small pieces
- 1 level tablespoon porridge oats
- 1 level tablespoon chopped mixed nuts
- ½ eating-apple, peeled, cored and chopped into small pieces
- ¼pt (150ml) (or less) warm milk
- runny honey for glaze

Preheat oven: Gas 6/400°F/200°C/fan oven 180°C
Position: above centre shelf
Baking time: about 25–40 minutes/fan oven about 22–26 minutes

Method: Put the yeast, sugar, flours, sultanas, apricots, oats, nuts and apple into a bowl. Mix well and pour in enough of the milk to make a soft dough. Knead for 2 or 3 minutes on a floured worktop and shape into a fat sausage. Have ready a greased 1lb (500g) loaf tin. Press the dough into it, filling the corners. Leave to rise in a warm place. When doubled in size, bake. Turn out of the tin and put on to a wire rack. Heat a tablespoon of honey in a small pan and brush the top of the loaf with it. Leave to grow cold. Serve sliced and buttered. Eat within 2 days and store as for bread.

Oat and Malt Loaf (makes 1 small loaf) ♡♡♡

Dark, sticky and fruity, this teabread is a treat. Ideal for tea or elevenses.

- 3 dessert-grade dates
- ¼pt (150ml) cold water
- 1 heaped tablespoon low-fat dried milk granules
- 2 teaspoons runny honey
- 1 generous tablespoon malt extract
- 1 tablespoon black treacle
- 2oz (50g) porridge oats
- 6oz (170g) plain flour (wholewheat or white unbleached, or a mixture)
- 1 heaped tablespoon baking powder
- ¼ teaspoon salt
- 1 tablespoon sunflower oil

Preheat oven: Gas 3/325°F/160°C/fan oven 140°C
Position: above centre shelf
Baking time: about 1 hour/fan oven 40 minutes

Method: Grease a 1lb (500g) loaf tin and line with greased greaseproof paper. Cut the dates in half and remove the stones, then cut into quarters and sprinkle with a little flour to stop the pieces sticking together. Put the water into a small saucepan with the dried milk. Stir until dissolved. Add the honey, malt and treacle. Heat gently while you stir, until evenly mixed and lukewarm. Grind the oats to flour in a coffee grinder. Put into a bowl with the plain flour, baking powder and salt. Mix well. Rub in the oil with the fingers. Add the dates and the liquid from the saucepan. Use a wooden spoon to mix to a soft dough, adding a little more milk if it is too stiff. Spoon into the prepared tin and press into the corners with a knife. Bake. Turn out on to a wire rack to cool. Leave the papers on until the bread is cut. Slice thinly and spread with butter or margarine. Store wrapped in an airtight container and use within 2 or 3 days. After the first day, nice toasted.

NOTE: Put the malt extract and black treacle in a warm place before using—this makes them easier to measure out.

Oat and Currant Bread (makes 1 small loaf) ♡♡

Slightly more substantial than ordinary currant bread. Serve sliced and buttered for tea or a snack. Store as you would bread.

2oz (50g) porridge oats
6oz (170g) strong white flour
level teaspoon mixed spice
1½oz (40g) polyunsaturated margarine
¼oz (7g) sachet instant 'fast action' yeast
1 slightly heaped tablespoon caster sugar
2oz (50g) currants
1 level teaspoon low-fat dried milk granules
4fl oz (125ml) lukewarm water
½ beaten egg
1 tablespoon melted honey for glaze

Preheat oven: Gas 7/425°F/220°C/fan oven 200°C
Position: centre shelf
Baking time: about 30 minutes/fan oven 20 minutes

Method: Grind the oats to flour in a coffee grinder. Put into a bowl with the other flour and the spice. Add the margarine and rub in with the fingertips. Sprinkle in the yeast, sugar and currants. Mix well to distribute evenly. Stir the dried milk into the water. Pour on to the flour mixture and add the egg. Mix by hand, pulling the mixture into 1 ball of dough. Knead on a floured worktop for 2 minutes, until smooth. Pick the dough up and slap it down hard on the worktop. Do this 3 times to activate the yeast. Have ready a greased 1lb (500g) loaf tin. Press the dough in with the knuckles, to fill the corners. Leave to rise in a warm place until doubled in size, then bake. Turn out of the tin. Have the glaze ready-warmed to brush over the top of the loaf. Leave to grow cold on a wire rack. Serve freshly baked, or toasted the following day.

NOTE: The loaf is done when it sounds hollow when knocked on the base.

Fruit and Oat Plait (serves 5 or 6) ♡♡♡

A plait of yeasted, sweetened bread encloses the fruit to make an impressive Danish pastry. Serve for elevenses, brunch or tea.

Dough

1oz (25g) polyunsaturated margarine
1oz (25g) porridge oats
3oz (75g) plain white or wholewheat flour
2 heaped teaspoons caster or soft brown sugar
¼ level teaspoon cinnamon
¼oz (7g) instant 'fast action' yeast
2½fl oz (75ml) warm milk
½ beaten egg
more flour for kneading

Filling

1oz (25g) polyunsaturated margarine, melted
½oz (15g) ground almonds
3 drops almond flavouring
1oz (25g) sultanas
½ large cooking-apple, coarsely grated
¼ level teaspoon cinnamon
1oz (25g) sugar
3 tablespoons fresh orange juice
1 heaped tablespoon porridge oats

Topping

2 heaped tablespoons icing sugar
1½–2 teaspoons water
about 1 tablespoon toasted flaked almonds

Preheat oven: Gas 8/450°F/230°C/fan oven 210°C
Position: top shelf
Baking time: 15 minutes/fan oven 12 minutes

Method: First prepare the dough. Melt the margarine gently in a small pan. Make the 1oz (25g) oats into flour, using a coffee grinder. Put into a mixing bowl with the plain flour, sugar, cinnamon and yeast. Stir, and make a well in the centre. Add the melted margarine, the milk and the egg. Mix to a paste using a fork, then knead lightly on a floured worktop. Roll out on a greased and floured baking sheet,

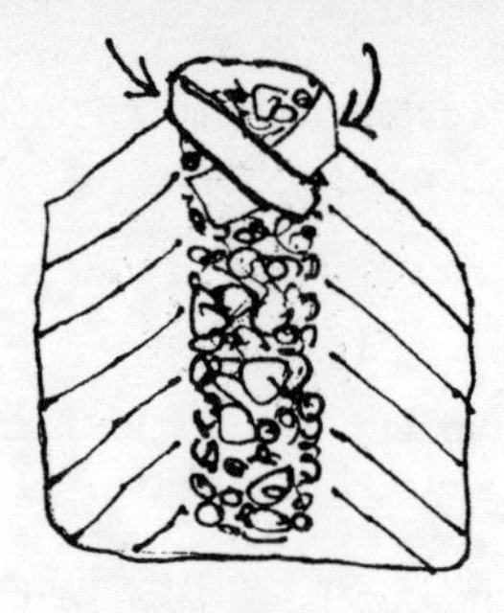

making an approximately 8 × 10in (20 × 25cm) rectangle.

Mix the filling ingredients in a basin. Spread down the centre of the pastry in a 2in (5cm) wide strip. Take a sharp knife and cut the pastry each side of the filling, as shown. Then fold the strips alternately over the filling, to form a plait. Neaten the two ends, to seal in the filling. Leave in a warm place for 15–20 minutes to double in size. Bake for 5 minutes then lower the heat to Gas 6/400°F/200°C/fan oven 180°C. Move down to the shelf above centre and continue baking for another 10 minutes. Leave to cool on the baking sheet for a few minutes. Mix the icing in a cup with enough water to make a thick but runny icing, then spread the top of the plait with the water icing and sprinkle with the almonds. Serve while still warm, cut into generous slices. Eat on the day of baking.

NOTE: Needs to be put into a hot oven so as to hold the shape of the plait.

Variations

- Fresh ripe apricots, peaches, plums or nectarines can be used in the filling—reduce the amount of apple by half, and replace with one of the above, having removed the stones and chopped it. All ingredients for the mixed filling should total 8oz (225g).

CHAPTER 9

Slices, Bars, Nibbles and Other Items

Date Slices (makes 20) ♡♡

These are high in fibre. The fruit can be varied—dried apricots soaked, stoned prunes, peaches, figs, pears, etc. A good lunchbox item, and suitable for elevenses, mid-afternoon break and tea, or as a snack.

Filling

1 tablespoon runny honey
juice of ½ lemon
3 tablespoons water
6oz (170g) chopped, stoned dates

Base

8oz (225g) plain wholewheat flour
4oz (100g) porridge oats
6oz (170g) polyunsaturated margarine
2oz (50g) soft brown sugar

Preheat oven: Gas 5/375°F/190°C/fan oven 170°C
Position: above centre shelf
Baking time: 35–40 minutes/fan oven 23–27 minutes

Method: Put the filling ingredients into a small saucepan. Heat through, then simmer while you stir until the dates have softened, adding more water if they go too dry (aim for a spreadable paste). Mix the flour and oats in a bowl. Add the margarine and rub in with the fingers until the mixture resembles large breadcrumbs. Stir in the sugar with a fork. Have ready a greased baking tray, 7 × 11in (18 × 27cm), lined with greased greaseproof paper. Use half the oat mixture to cover the baking tray, pressing it down well. Spread with the date paste and sprinkle the remaining oat mixture over the top as evenly as you can. Press firmly. Bake. Allow to cool a little in the tin, then cut into 20 bars. Leave in the tin to grow cold. Take out carefully and store in an airtight container. Eat within 3 or 4 days.

Flapjacks (makes 12) ♡

One of the classic oat recipes. Golden brown and chewy.

2oz (50g) polyunsaturated margarine
2oz (50g) golden syrup
4oz (100g) demerara sugar
6oz (170g) rolled oats

Preheat oven: Gas 4/350°F/180°C/fan oven 160°C
Position: top shelf
Baking time: 20 minutes/fan oven

Method: Put the margarine, syrup and sugar into a saucepan and set over a gentle heat. Stir with a wooden spoon to combine, while the margarine melts and the sugar dissolves. Take off the heat and stir in the oats. Have ready an 8in (20cm) square tin. Spread the mixture over the base and use a metal spoon to flatten it evenly. Bake until golden brown. Leave to cool in the tin for 5 minutes, then cut into 12 pieces with a sharp knife (make sure you cut right through). Leave in the tin to grow cold. Remove with a spatula and store in an airtight container.

Variations

- *Groat Flapjacks*: Instead of all porridge oats use 3oz (75g) whole oats (groats) and 3oz (75g) porridge oats.
- *Honey Flapjacks*: Instead of golden syrup use runny honey.
- *Nut Flapjacks*: Instead of all porridge oats use 5oz (135g) porridge oats and 1oz (25g) chopped nuts. Almonds, cashews, walnuts, brazils and hazelnuts are all suitable.
- *Chocolate Flapjacks*: Sift 1 heaped teaspoon cocoa powder into the saucepan with the margarine, syrup and sugar.
- *Sesame Flapjacks*: After flattening the uncooked mixture sprinkle with sesame seeds.

Dark Flapjacks: Instead of all golden syrup, use 1oz (25g) black treacle and 1oz (25g) golden syrup.

- *Sunflower-seed Flapjacks*: Instead of all oats use 5oz (135g) porridge oats and 1oz (25g) sunflower seeds.

Oat, Fruit and Nut Fingers (makes 12) ♡♡

These are flapjacks with a vengeance! They are extra-chewy, oaty, fruity and nutty—just the thing for your elevenses or afternoon break. The base is always the same, but the nuts and fruit can be varied according to what is in the cupboard.

3oz (75g) polyunsaturated margarine
1½oz (40g) soft brown sugar
1 generous tablespoon golden syrup
4oz (100g) porridge oats
1½oz (40g) shelled nuts (see below)
2oz (50g) dried fruit (see below)

Preheat oven: Gas 4/350°F/180°C/fan oven 160°C
Position: above centre shelf
Baking time: about 40 minutes/fan oven about 25 minutes

Method: Put the margarine, sugar, and syrup in a saucepan. Set over a gentle heat while you stir. When the margarine has melted and the sugar dissolved, take off the heat and stir in the oats. Chop the nuts and fruit quite small on a chopping board. Add to the saucepan and stir in. Have ready a greased 7½in (19cm) square sponge tin lined with greased greaseproof paper. Turn the mixture into it and spread flat with the back of a metal spoon, dipped in cold water. Bake until golden brown. Leave to cool in the tin for 3 minutes. Smear the blade of a sharp knife with margarine and cut the baked mixture into 12 fingers, making sure you cut right through. Leave in the tin to grow cold and crisp before removing with a knife. Store in an airtight container. Use within a week.

Nuts
Almonds, cashews, hazelnuts and walnuts are all suitable. Try just one kind, or a mixture.

Dried fruit
Sultanas, raisins, apricots, peaches and pears are all suitable. Use 1 or 2 kinds or a mixture, according to what is in the cupboard. Chop them all—even the sultanas and raisins.

Oat Nibbles (makes about 50) ♡♡♡

The huge commercial snack/nibble market uses mainly potatoes, corn and wheat with a good deal of fat and salt, not to mention artificial additives, colourings, flavourings, 'enhancers' and heaven knows what else. Avoid all these, and be thrifty too, by making your own moreish and much healthier versions at home. Here is a quick new recipe based on oats with a variety of flavours to tempt everyone.

Basic dough

- 2 heaped tablespoons porridge oats
- 1 heaped teaspoon Parmesan cheese, finely grated
- ½ level teaspoon made French mustard
- 2 tablespoons milk
- flavouring of your choice (see below)

Preheat oven: Gas 7/425°F/220°C/fan oven 200°C

Position: top shelf
Baking time: about 7 minutes/fan oven about 5 minutes

Method: Use a teaspoon to mix all the ingredients in a basin to a sticky paste. Taste, and correct the flavouring if necessary. Have ready a greased baking sheet. Using two teaspoons together, place ¼ teaspoons of the paste on to it, leaving space around each one. Flatten and spread out each with the back of a spoon. The shapes will be irregular, which is characteristic of these little nibbles. Bake until brown around the edges. Take out of the oven and leave to cool on the baking sheet—as they cool down they will become crisp. Serve in small dishes to hand round with drinks. You can bag them up and seal them in small quantities for school, as part of a packed lunch. When cold, they can be stored in an airtight tin. Once they have been stored, they may need re-crisping in a hot oven for a couple of minutes.

NOTE: If you find these too small and fiddly to arrange on the baking sheet, make 12 larger ones and cut into quarters after baking, to make tiny fan shapes. They may need a little more baking time than the small ones.

Flavours
Add *one* of the following to the basic ingredients before mixing, adding a little more milk if the paste turns out too stiff, or a few more oats if it looks too wet.

Bacon—½ rasher lean bacon grilled until really crisp, then broken into small pieces and pounded to a paste with a pestle and mortar
Cheese—1 extra level teaspoon Parmesan cheese, finely grated
Garlic—1 medium-sized clove garlic put through a crusher
Hot—1 good pinch cayenne pepper, or more
Hot spice—2 good pinches curry powder, or more
Italian—¼ level teaspoon tomato purée, 1 good pinch dried basil

Tomato—½ level teaspoon tomato purée and 2 pinches caster sugar

Cheese and Oat Cocktail Biscuits (makes about 20) ♡♡♡

Crisp little golden biscuits with a bold taste. Ideal for serving with drinks.

1oz (25g) porridge oats
1oz (25g) plain white flour
¾oz (20g) polyunsaturated margarine
1oz (25g) mashed potato
1oz (25g) tasty Cheddar cheese, finely grated
½ teaspoon made French mustard
1 tablespoon water

Preheat oven: Gas 7/425°F/220°C/fan oven 200°C
Position: top shelf
Baking time: 10–12 minutes/fan oven 8 minutes

Method: Put the oats and flour into a bowl. Add the margarine and rub in with the fingertips until the mixture resembles bread-crumbs. Put in the mashed potato and rub in. Add the cheese, mustard and water. Pull together by hand into 1 ball. Knead on a floured worktop for a minute, until smooth and heavy. Roll out thinly and cut into rounds with a fluted cutter, size 2in (5cm) diameter. Place the rounds on a baking sheet dusted with flour and prick with a fork. Bake until crisp and golden. Cool on a wire rack. When cold, store in an airtight container. Re-crisp in the oven for two minutes before serving. Eat within a few days.

NOTE: If you would prefer smaller biscuits, cut each one into quarters with a sharp knife to make 4 fan-shaped nibbles. Alternatively, cut out with a smaller cutter and bake for less time.

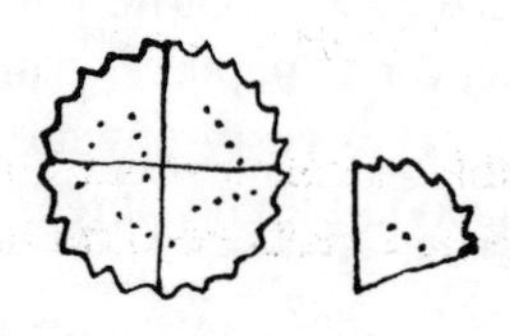

Savoury Crunchies (makes 2 bowls of nibbles) ♡♡♡

After baking, there is absolutely no sign of the oats except for the crunchy texture. Eat these tasty nibbles freshly baked, served with drinks.

Pastry

1oz (25g) plain white flour
1oz (25g) plain wholewheat flour
1oz (25g) polyunsaturated margarine
1½ tablespoons cold water

Filling

1oz (25g) porridge oats
1oz (25g) tasty Cheddar cheese, finely grated
1oz (25g) polyunsaturated margarine
1 teaspoon made mustard
milk for brushing

Preheat oven: Gas 6/400°F/200°C/fan oven 180°C
Position: top shelf
Baking time: about 20 minutes/fan oven about 14 minutes

Method: First make the pastry. Put the two flours into a bowl. Mix well and rub in the margarine until the mixture resembles breadcrumbs. Add the water and mix by hand to a soft dough. Flour the worktop and knead the dough lightly for a few seconds. Roll out thinly into a circle. Now make the filling. Mix the oats, cheese, melted margarine and mustard in a basin. Brush the pasty with milk, all over. Spread half with the filling, not quite to the edge, and fold the other half over to cover it. Roll out thinly, pressing the edges to seal. Put on to a baking sheet and prick all over with a fork. Bake until crisp and golden. Cool for a minute and put on to a chopping board. With a large, really sharp knife, cut into thin strips and then short lengths. Put into 2 serving bowls to grow cold. Pass round with drinks as an appetiser.

Fruit and Oat Nibbles (makes about 20) ♡

These quickly prepared sweets need no baking. Eat as a treat.

¾oz (20g) polyunsaturated margarine
¾oz (20g) soft brown sugar
2 tablespoons golden syrup
2 heaped tablespoons chopped dried fruit (see below)
1oz (25g) porridge oats

Method: Put the margarine, sugar and golden syrup into a saucepan. Set over a gentle heat while you stir, to dissolve the sugar and melt the margarine. Increase the heat and bring to the boil. Now reduce the heat and simmer for 4 minutes. Take off the hob and add the prepared fruit and oats. Stir until all the liquid has been absorbed. Use 2 teaspoons together to make small heaps of the mixture on a baking sheet lined with baking parchment. Leave to set, then wrap in food film individually, like sweets. Store in a jar or sweet tin and eat within 2 days.

Dried fruit
Use a mixture of any three of the following dried/ready-to-eat fruit:

apricots
mango
pawpaw
peaches
pears
pineapple
raisins
sultanas

STUFFING

Traditionally cooks used to stuff the cavities of poultry to keep them moist and to absorb the cooking juices. This is no longer thought to be good practice because of the risk of salmonella and the possibility that neither the inside of the poultry nor the stuffing will reach a high enough temperature. Nowadays the trend is to leave the cavity empty and cook the stuffing in a separate dish or tin.

Stuffing can have a variety of flavours, and can be as soft or crisp as desired. It can be served with roast meat such as pork, or a vegetarian nut roast. Stuffing should enhance the main source of protein in the meal. It should not be so bold in appearance or flavour as to challenge the meat etc.—rather, it should complement it and add to its flavour.

Oat Stuffing (4 servings) ♡♡♡♡

- 1½ slices bread, made into crumbs
- 2 level teaspoons chopped fresh mixed herbs, or 1 level teaspoon dried
- 2 tablespoons porridge oats
- ½ medium onion, finely chopped
- 1 tablespoon sunflower oil
- salt and freshly ground black pepper to taste
- cold water

Method: Mix all the ingredients in a basin, adding enough water to make a sloppy paste. Turn into a shallow greased ovenproof dish and spread flat with a knife. Bake until firm, crisp and browning round the edge, if that is the way you like it. In a hot oven on the top shelf it will be crisp in 25 minutes/ fan oven 16 minutes. Alternatively, if you prefer it soft, put it in the oven at the same time as the joint or poultry, etc. and take it out when it is done, keeping it hot until ready to serve. In a slow oven on the top shelf it will take about 40 minutes/ fan oven 26 minutes to bake. Leftover stuffing can be served cold with cold meat or used in meat sandwiches, sliced thinly.

Oat Stuffing with Lemon and Parsley ♡♡♡♡

Make as for oat stuffing, but omit the mixed herbs. Instead, add the finely grated rind of ½ lemon and 1 heaped tablespoon chopped fresh parsley. Serve with chicken or a nut roast.

Oat, Orange and Walnut Stuffing ♡♡♡

Make as for oat stuffing, but omit the mixed herbs. Instead, add the finely grated rind of ½ an orange, 1 heaped teaspoon chopped parsley and 6 chopped walnut halves. Also add the juice of ½ an orange. Serve with turkey or chicken.

Oat, Sage and Onion Stuffing ♡♡♡♡

Make as for oat stuffing. Omit the mixed herbs, and instead add 1 heaped teaspoon finely chopped fresh sage, or

1 level teaspoon dried sage, with a little more finely chopped onion.

NOTE: For a crisp *dry* stuffing (which some prefer), add less water to the mixture.

Oat Yorkshire Puddings (makes 8 small) ♡♡♡

Slightly more substantial than the usual variety, but light and much lower in fat.

2 teaspoons sunflower oil
½oz (15g) porridge oats
1½oz (40g) white plain flour
1 pinch salt
1 medium egg
2 tablespoons milk
2½ tablespoons water

Preheat oven: Gas 7/425°F/220°C/fan oven 200°C
Position: top shelf
Baking time: 15 minutes/fan oven 10 minutes

Method: Use a screw of kitchen paper to grease 8 patty tins with the oil. Put into the oven on the top shelf while you make the batter. Grind the oats to flour, using a coffee grinder. Put into a bowl with the plain flour and salt and mix well. Using a fork, whisk the egg and milk in a basin. Pour into the flours and mix/beat well until creamy. Stir in the water to make a thin batter. Take the hot patty tins out of the oven. Spoon a tablespoon of batter into each one and put back into the oven. Bake until well risen, crisp and golden. Serve with traditional roast beef or vegetarian nut roast, vegetables and gravy.

NOTE: Take care when handling the patty tins—they will become very hot.

Oat Dumplings (makes 6 small) ♡♡♡

Usually, dumplings are made with wheat flour and suet to give them their characteristic texture. These are different as they don't contain suet but do contain oats—which makes them low in cholesterol but gives them the correct texture.

1oz (25g) porridge oats
2oz (50g) white self-raising flour
¼ level teaspoon baking powder
salt and freshly ground black pepper
1oz (25g) polyunsaturated margarine
2 tablespoons cold water

Method: Grind the oats to flour in a coffee grinder. Put into a bowl with the self-raising flour, baking powder and seasoning to taste. Mix well and add the margarine. Rub in with the fingertips until the mixture resembles coarse breadcrumbs. Add the water and mix to a soft dough with a fork. With floured hands break off walnut-sized pieces and roll into balls between the palms. Put into stews or casseroles for the last 20 minutes of cooking. The dumplings will increase in size and become soft and moist.

Variations

- Add ¼ level teaspoon mixed dried herbs with the flour.
- Add 1 tablespoon freshly chopped parsley with the flour.

Lemon Brose ♡♡♡♡

This is what children drank before there was 'pop' and as an alternative to lemon barley water. It is more satisfying than plain lemonade and the oatmeal makes it more nutritious.

2oz (50g) medium oatmeal
1 slightly heaped tablespoon soft brown sugar
1 lemon, washed
½pt (300ml) boiling water

Method: Mix the oatmeal and sugar in a large heat-proof jug. Cut the lemon in half. Squeeze the juice from each half including pips into the jug. Put in the pieces of lemon and pour the boiling water over. Give the mixture a good stir, cover with a clean tea-towel and leave to cool down. When cold, strain through a fine-mesh sieve, pressing the lemon pieces with the back of a wooden spoon to squeeze out all the juice. Thin down with cold water and serve. Best drunk within 24 hours of making.

Notes

CHOICE OF FLOUR

In the recipes you will find *plain*, *self-raising* and *strong* flours used. These are available as white, unbleached white and wholewheat flours. People inclined to wholefoods will prefer to use wholewheat flour (brown) as it contains more fibre than white flour. Others will prefer the unbleached white to the bleached white flour. Some people like to use white flour because they find wholewheat too difficult to digest. Unbleached white flour is difficult to find in some areas. Organic flours are gaining popularity, both white and brown, for their flavour and purity.

Whichever kind of flour you personally choose to use, make sure it matches the recipe suggestion—plain, self-raising or strong. Where a recipe depends on wholewheat, white or unbleached white flour it is specified.

Strong flour

This is sometimes called 'bread flour' or 'pasta flour'. It has a higher gluten content than ordinary flour and is used for bread and pasta. It is not really suitable for cakes, pastry, biscuits and cookies as it will make them too tough. Strong flour is available as white or brown but only plain.

Wholewheat flour (plain and self-raising)

This is used for robust baking of the 'farmhouse' type. It requires extra liquid to prevent results being too dry and heavy. This is due to the bran content. If this is the flour of your choice, please adjust liquid to suit.

Plain flour

This is finely ground flour with less fibre and gluten than wholewheat. It is very white if bleached during manufacture. Buy unbleached if you can. It will be a pale cream colour but less processed. Both types are soft flours suitable for baking biscuits and pastry. They can be used for bread and pasta but will make a weaker dough than strong flour.

Self-raising flour

This is plain flour but with raising agents added. Bicarbonate of soda and cream of tartar are the usual additives. Mainly used for cakes where a light texture is required.

FRUIT PEEL

While one school of thought suggests leaving the peel on fruit such as apples and pears, to be eaten as 'wholefood', another school of thought is in favour of peeling off the skin to counteract husbandry methods such as spraying with chemicals. It really comes down to personal preference.

PEANUTS

Peanuts, which have a bad reputation with allergy sufferers, are not really nuts at all. They are actually a kind of bean. They are widely used in the manufacture of foods as they are cheap and look exactly like nuts. They are used as a base for mixed chopped nuts for cooking. Best avoided.

YEAST

For the yeasted bread, rolls, buns etc. throughout this book a special kind of yeast is used—instant 'fast action' dried yeast. It is sold in 7g and 15g sachets (usually in boxes of 6 or 8) and has vitamin C (ascorbic acid) added to make it work very quickly—it requires only one rising. Ordinary 'instant' dried yeast does not share this extra ingredient and will work more slowly, requiring two risings, although, like the 'fast action' kind, it can be added dry to the flour. Fresh yeast and dried yeast (granules), on the other hand, need to be mixed with warm water and, with a little sugar, encouraged to 'work'. They cannot be added dry to the flour.

As the names of the yeasts tend to be confusing, it is wise to consult the instructions on the packet. If they tell you to add the yeast straight to the flour and that only one rising is needed, it will be instant 'fast action' dried yeast in the packet. Buy it at supermarkets and grocery stores.

Important: If you use fresh, dried or ordinary 'instant' yeast you will need an extra rising of the dough for the recipes.

Fresh yeast
Use double the amount given in the recipe. Cream with a little warm water and a teaspoon of sugar. Leave in a warm place until frothy, then use instead of instant 'fast action' yeast. Allow for two risings.

Dried yeast (granules)
Sprinkle into 3 tablespoons of warm water. Add 1 teaspoon of sugar and leave in a warm place to soften and grow frothy. Use instead of instant 'fast action' dried yeast. Allow for two risings instead of one.

Instant dried yeast
Mix dry into the flour. Use in the same way as instant 'fast action' yeast, but allow for two risings instead of one.

Brewer's yeast
Unsuitable for baking, as it is not live.

CONVERSION TABLES

Liquid measures

The average UK tea cup contains ¼pt (150ml). The American measuring cup is two-fifths of a UK pint as the American pint is slightly smaller than a UK pint (UK pint = 20fl oz, American pint = 16fl oz).

Solid measures

American cup conversions

1 cup breadcrumbs = 4oz (100g)
1 cup butter, margarine = 8oz (225g)
1 cup cheese, grated = 4oz (100g)
1 cup flour = 4oz (100g)
1 cup caster sugar = 7oz (200g)

Spoon conversions

½oz flour = 1 level tablespoon
1oz flour = 1 heaped tablespoon
1oz sugar = 1 level tablespoon
½oz butter = 1 levelled off tablespoon
1oz jam = 1 level tablespoon

FAN OVENS

As fan ovens vary from model to model, please consult the manufacturer's instructions regarding temperature settings. All the recipes in this book suggest 20°C lower than conventional oven settings and one third less baking time. This may not apply to all fan ovens.

Index

The following symbols have been used after entries for recipes to denote suitability for different diets:

C = suitable for coeliacs who are allowed oats. These recipes do not contain wheat, rye or barley, or their gluten. **Coeliacs should not eat oats unless they have received medical advice to do so.**

EF = egg-free

V = vegetarian. If cheese is used in the recipes, vegetarian cheese made without rennet should be used.

WF = wheat-free

	C	EF	V	WF
fruit – continued				
peel 131				
salad and oat cake 101–2			•	
gourmet porridge 31	•	•	•	•
Granola 38		•	•	
groats 7				
ham and mushroom pizza 58		•		
healthy diet *see* diet				
heart grading 25–6				
herrings in oatmeal 47–8	•	•		•
ice cream 67–9	•		•	•
instant oats 8				
jumbo oats 8				
leek and cheese pancake 49			•	
leek and oatmeal soup 46		•	•	
leek and potato pizza 57		•	•	
lemon brose 129	•	•	•	•
lumps in porridge 30				
malted brown oatbread 90–91		•	•	
malted oat breakfast flakes 29		•	•	•
meat				
beef rissoles 60				
chicken pancake 50				
chicken rissoles 60				
ham and mushroom pizza 58		•		

	C	EF	V	WF
oat and sesame biscuits 79–80	•		•	•
oat sponge buns 111–13			•	
oat stuffing 127–8		•	•	
oat and treacle bread 113–14		•	•	
oatcakes 98–9		•	•	
oatflakes 7–8				
oaties 27–8	•	•	•	•
oatmeal 7				
oatmeal biscuits 95			•	
oatmeal porridge 31–2	•	•	•	•
oats				
as a beauty aid 5				
characteristics of 3–4				
and the coeliac 4				
horse sense 9				
as medicine 4–5				
nutrition and energy 3–6				
popularity decline 5–6				
as prison fare 6				
products 6–8				
and sex 5				
shopping and storage 8–9				
wheat, comparison with 2				
see also diet				
onion, bacon and rosemary pizza 58		•		
orange oatmeal biscuits 77–8		•	•	
pancakes				
fruit fillings 42–3	•	•	•	•
oat 42–3			•	
prawn 50				
savoury oat 49–50				

	C	EF	V	WF
pancakes – continued				
sweet oat 73			•	
parkin 103–4			•	
pasta, oat 53–4			•	
pastry 63–4		•	•	
peanuts 131				
pizza, British style oat 56–8		•		
pork rissoles 61				
pork sausages, skinless and oat 43		•		
porridge				
chocolate 32	•	•	•	•
gourmet 31	•	•	•	•
lumps in 30				
microwave 31	•	•	•	•
oatmeal 31–2	•	•	•	•
oats 7				
plain 31–2	•	•	•	•
quick 31	•	•	•	•
raw fruit (muesli) 33	•	•	•	•
potassium 3, 22				
potato, mashed 52	•	•	•	•
prawn pancake 50				
prison fare 6				
quiche pastry, oat 64		•	•	
quick oat rolls 87–8		•	•	
quick oats 7–8				
quick porridge 31	•	•	•	•
rhubarb oat crumble 74–5		•	•	
rolled oats 7–8				
rolls *see* bread and rolls				

	C	EF	V	WF
salmon pancakes, fresh 50				
salt 21–2				
sardine fishcakes 60				
sausages				
oat 50–51			●	
skinless pork and oat 43–4		●		
savoury cakes with oat coating 58–62				
savoury crunchies 125		●	●	
savoury oat pancakes 49–50				
savoury pie with oat pastry 61–2				
scones				
cheese and oat 92–3		●	●	
fruit and oat 93–4		●	●	
oat and apple 92		●	●	
oat drop 94–5			●	
sesame oat crispbreads 98		●	●	
shortcrust pastry, oat 63–4		●	●	
small oats 8				
soft oat bread 88		●	●	
soups				
asparagus with oats 45–6		●	●	
chicken, oat and vegetables 47		●		
leek and oatmeal 46		●	●	
spicy oat crumble 71–2		●	●	
stuffing 126–8		●	●	
sugar 13				
superfast oats 7–8				
sweet oat pastry 64		●	●	
toasted muesli 36–7	●	●	●	●
treacle tart 64–5		●	●	

	C	EF	V	WF
trout in oatmeal 48	•	•		•
tuna fishcakes 60				
vanilla oat wafers 84–5		•	•	
vegetable and oat rissoles 52–3			•	
vegetarian cottage pie with oats 52		•	•	
vegetarian oat rissoles 51		•	•	
vegetarian oat roast 52		•	•	
vegetarian rissoles 61			•	
vitamins 3, 17–20				
water in diet 23				
West Country oat buns 109–10			•	
white sauce, basic 49	•	•	•	•
whitebait in oat flour 48	•	•		•
yeast 131–2				
Yorkshire pudding, oat 128			•	

The symbols in this index used after entries for recipes denote their suitability for different diets:
C = suitable for coeliacs who are allowed oats. These recipes do not contain wheat, rye or barley, or their gluten. **Coeliacs should not eat oats unless they have received medical advice to do so.**
EF = egg-free
V = vegetarian. If cheese is used in the recipes, vegetarian cheese made without rennet should be used.
WF = wheat-free